K Selman

De Gaulle and Twentieth-Century France

De Gaulle and Twentieth-Century France

Edited by

Hugh Gough and John Horne

Edward Arnold
A member of the Hodder Headline Group
LONDON NEW YORK MELBOURNE AUCKLAND

© 1994 selection and editorial matter John Horne and Hugh Gough

First published in Great Britain 1994

Distributed in the USA by Routledge, Chapman and Hall, Inc.
29 West 35th Street, New York, NY 10001

British Library Cataloguing in Publication Data

Available on request

ISBN 0-340-58826-8

Origination by GreenGate Publishing Services, Tonbridge, Kent
Printed and bound in Great Britain for Edward Arnold,
a division of Hodder Headline plc,
338 Euston Road, London NW1 3BH,
by Biddles Ltd, Guildford and King's Lynn

Contents

Preface

This book is made up of the papers presented at a conference held in the Alliance Française in Dublin, in November 1990, to mark the centenary of the birth of Charles de Gaulle. The conference was organized by the Alliance Française de Dublin, the Department of Modern History of Trinity College Dublin and the Department of Modern History of University College Dublin.

The conference itself would never have come about without the enthusiastic support of the then *délégué général* of the Alliance Française, Monsieur Rémy Durand, who provided much of the necessary financial and organizational assistance. We are grateful to him, and to the generous help provided by his successor, Monsieur Michel Carrière. Brigitte Lemoine, also of the Alliance Française, provided us with constant support throughout. The translations of the French texts were carried out by Ms Cathérine Burke and by Dr Darach Sanfey. Financial assistance towards publication was provided by the Alliance Française, the Department of Modern History of Trinity College Dublin, and the Academic Publications Committee of University College Dublin. We would like to express our thanks to them all, and not least to our contributors, for making this publication possible. Finally, we would like to thank Christopher Wheeler and the editorial team at Edward Arnold for their encouragement and help.

Hugh Gough (University College Dublin)
John Horne (Trinity College Dublin)

Editors' Note

As this book is intended for a general readership and for student use, all French quotations have been translated into English except for certain footnotes in the contributions of Douglas Johnson and Robert Pickering, where the original French version was essential to the meaning of the text. Footnote references to French books refer to the English translation where one is available, but the date of the original French version is also given in the brackets which follow the title. This will enable readers to trace the French version where required.

Notes on the Contributors

The Contributors

François Bédarida has taught at the Institut Français in London, and at the Faculté des Lettres and the Institut d'Etudes Politiques in Paris. He was Director of the Institut d'Histoire du Temps Présent, Paris, from 1979 to 1991 and is a former General Secretary of the International Committee of Historical Sciences. Recent works include *La Bataille d'Angleterre* (1985); (with others) *Normandie 44: du débarquement à la Libération* (1987); (with others) *La politique nazie d'extermination* (1989); *Le Nazisme et le génocide* (1989), and *A Social History of England, 1851–1990* (new ed. 1991).

Serge Berstein has taught at the Université de Paris X (Nanterre) and since 1985 at the Institut d'Etudes Politiques, Paris. He is a co-founder with Pierre Milza of the Centre d'Histoire de l'Europe du XXe siècle. His publications include *Histoire du parti radical* (2 vols., 1980–2); *Edouard Herriot ou la République en personne* (1985); *La France des années trente* (1988); and Volumes 12 and 17 in the Nouvelle Histoire de la France contemporaine: (with J.-J. Becker) *Victoire et frustration, 1914–1929* (1990); and *La France de l'expansion*, vol. 1, *La République gaullienne* (1989).

Julian Jackson was educated at the University of Cambridge and has been a lecturer since 1983 in the University College of Swansea. He has published *The Politics of Depression in France 1932–1936* (1985); *The Popular Front in France 1934–1938* (1988); and *De Gaulle* (1990). He is currently working on a history of France, 1914–1989.

Douglas Johnson was educated at the University of Oxford and as a foreign student at the Ecole Normale Supérieure, Paris. He was Professor of Modern History at the University of Birmingham and subsequently Professor of French History, University College, London. Publications include *France and the Dreyfus Affair* (1966); *The French Revolution* (1970); (with F. Bédarida and F. Crouzet), *De Guillaume le Conquérant au marché commun: dix siècles d'histoire franco-britannique* (1979); (with Madeleine Johnson), *The Age of Illusion: Art and Politics in France 1918–1940* (1987); (with G. Best), *The Permanent Revolution* (1988); and *Michelet and the French Revolution* (1990).

Jean-Marie Mayeur was educated in Strasbourg and Paris. He has taught at the Université de Lyon II and the Université de Paris XII (Val-de-Marne), and since 1981 at the Université de Paris IV. Since 1974, he has been Professor at the Institut d'Etudes Politiques, Paris. From 1978 to 1983 he was Director of the Institut d'Histoire Moderne et Contemporaine. Publications include *La Séparation de l'église et de l'état* (1966); *Un Prêtre démocratique, l'abbé Lemire 1853–1928* (1968); *Autonomie et politique en Alsace. La Constitution de 1911* (1970); (with M. Rebérioux), *The Third Republic from its origins to the Great War, 1871–1914* (1984); and *Catholicisme social et démocratie chrétienne. Principes romains, expériences françaises* (1986).

Robert Pickering was educated at the Universities of Melbourne and Oxford. He has taught at Trinity College, Dublin and Downing College, Cambridge. Since 1983, he has been Professor of French at University College, Cork and is currently also Professeur Associé à la section des lettres modernes, Universités de Clermont II and Paris XII. He is a member of research teams on the work of Paul Valéry at the CNRS and the Institut des Textes et Manuscrits Modernes. He is the author of articles and books on nineteenth- and twentieth-century French literature, including *Lautréamont-Ducasse: Image, Theme and Self-Identity* (1990).

René Rémond was Professor of Contemporary History at the Université de Paris X (Nanterre) from 1964 to 1986, and at the Institut d'Etudes Politiques from 1968 to 1986. He has been Director of Studies and Research at the Fondation Nationale des Sciences Politiques since 1956, and President since 1981. First President of the Université de Paris X, and first Vice-President of the Conférence des Présidents d'Université (1974–5), he was also President of the Commission du Xe Plan Enseignement-Formation, and has been President of the Commission Supérieure des Archives since 1988. In addition to frequent appearances on radio and television programmes concerning historical matters and current affairs, he has published numerous articles and some twenty-five books on the political, intellectual and religious history of nineteenth- and twentieth-century France, including *The Right Wing in France from 1815 to De Gaulle* (1968); *La Règle et le consentement* (1979); *Les Catholiques dans la France des années 30* (1979); *Le Retour de De Gaulle* (1987); and *Notre Siècle* (1988). Works that he has edited include *Le programme commun de la résistance* (1984) and *Pour une histoire politique* (1988).

Jean-Pierre Rioux is a former Director of Research at the Institut d'Histoire du Temps Présent (CNRS), Paris, and editor of *Vingtième Siècle: Revue d'histoire*. Member of the editorial committees of *L'Histoire* and *Le Mouvement social*, he is also the author of an historical column in *Le Monde*. He has published widely on the cultural and political history of contemporary France, including *La Révolution industrielle 1780–1880* (1971); *Révolutionnaires du Front Populaire* (1973); *Nationalisme et conservatisme. La Ligue de la Patrie Française* (1977); and *The Fourth Republic, 1944–1958* (1987). He has recently edited *La Guerre d'Algérie et les français* (1990) and *La Vie culturelle sous Vichy* (1990).

Michel Winock is Professor of Contemporary History at the Institut d'Etudes Politiques. A member of the editorial committee of *Vingtième siècle: Revue d'histoire*, and a regular contributor to *Le Monde*, *L'Evénement du Jeudi*, and *L'Histoire*, his publications include *Histoire politique de la revue Esprit, 1930–1950* (1975); *La République se meurt, chronique 1956–1958* (1978); *La Fièvre hexagonale. Les grandes crises politiques en France 1871–1968* (1968); *Chronique des années soixante* (1987); *1789, l'année sans pareille* (1990); *Nationalisme, antisémitisme et fascisme en France* (1990); and (with J.-F. Sirinelli) *La Guerre d'Algérie et les intellectuels français* (1991).

The Editors

Hugh Gough was educated at the University of Oxford and is statutory lecturer in History at University College, Dublin. He has published many articles on the history of the French Revolution, is author of *The Newspaper Press in the French Revolution* (1988) and co-editor of *The Huguenots and Ireland. Anatomy of an Emigration* (1987) and *Ireland and the French Revolution* (1990).

John Horne was educated at the Universities of Oxford and Sussex. He is a senior lecturer in Modern European History and the Director of European Studies at Trinity College Dublin. He has published numerous articles on French labour and social history and on the comparative history of the First World War. He is the author of *Labour at War: France and Britain, 1914–1918* (1991).

List of Abbreviations

BCRA Bureau Central de Renseignement et d'Action – Central Office of Information and Action: Free French Intelligence Service: organized by Captain Dewavrin, 'Passy'

CFLN Comité Français de Libération Nationale – French Committee for National Liberation: established in Algiers 3 June 1943; became Provisional Government of the French Republic (GPRF) on 3 June 1944

CGT Confédération Générale du Travail – General Confederation of Labour: trade union confederation founded in 1895, dominated by communists since Second World War

CID–UNATI Comité d'Information et de Défense–Union Nationale des Artisans et Travailleurs Indépendants – Committee of Information and Defence–National Union of Artisans and Independent Workers: organization representing shopkeepers and small producers

CNR Conseil National de la Résistance – National Council of the Resistance: established in May 1943 by Jean Moulin, under the authority of de Gaulle, to represent internal resistance movements and the political formations and trade unions which supported them

FFI Forces Françaises de l'Intérieur – French Forces of the Interior: army formed in April 1944 from various resistance groups

FGDS

Fédération de la Gauche Démocratique et Socialiste – Federation of the Democratic and Socialist Left: set up on 10 September 1965 by François Mitterrand to co-ordinate parties and political clubs of the non-communist left; collapsed in the aftermath of the events of May 1968

FLN

Front de Libération Nationale – National Liberation Front: revolutionary guerilla organization founded in Algeria in October 1954

FTP

Francs-Tireurs et Partisans– Communist armed resistance organization during Second World War, active from 1941 onwards; joined by many non-communists as well

GPRA

Gouvernement Provisoire de la République Algérienne – Provisional Government of the Algerian Republic: founded in September 1959 in Cairo as a government in exile, with Ferhat Abbas as its first president

GPRF

Gouvernement Provisoire de la République Française – Provisional Government of the French Republic: established by de Gaulle 3 June 1944 (see CFLN above) as the provisional government for liberated France

MNA

Mouvement Nationaliste Algérien – Algerian Nationalist Movement: Algerian nationalist party founded by Messali Hadj in 1954 as a successor to his previous party (MTLD); most members quickly defected to the FLN, or were eliminated by it. Virtually defunct by early 1960s

MRP

Mouvement Républicain Populaire – Popular Republican Movement: liberal Catholic party founded in 1944 and influential in the early governments of the Fourth Republic

OAS

Organisation de l'Armée Secrète – Organization of the Secret Army: terrorist organization founded in February 1961 by civilians and military deserters in France and Algeria to resist Algerian independence

OCM	Organisation Civile et Militaire – Civil and Military Organisation: resistance movement in the German-occupied part of France, supported mainly by higher civil servants and business leaders
PCF	Parti Communiste Français – French Communist Party: founded at the Socialist Party congress at Tours in December 1920, when a majority of delegates sympathetic to the Russian revolution voted to affiliate to the Third International
RPF	Rassemblement du Peuple Français – Gathering of the French People: political movement launched by de Gaulle in April 1947, for reform of the constitution of the Fourth Republic. Disbanded in 1953
RPR	Rassemblement pour la République – Gathering for the Republic: see UNR below
SFIO	Section Française de l'Internationale Ouvrière – French Section of the Workers' International: French Socialist Party founded in1905; merged into new Parti Socialiste in 1969
SOE	Special Operations Executive – secret British organisation in the Second World War which liaised with resistance groups and sent in trained saboteurs to assist them
STO	Service du Travail Obligatoire – Obligatory Labour Service: created by Laval in February 1943, to provide French workers for Germany for the war effort
UNR	Union pour la Nouvelle République – Union for the New Republic: Gaullist party founded in October 1958 to fight the November elections of that year; name later changed to UDVe (Union des Démocrates pour la Cinquième République) in 1967, to UDR (Union des Démocrates pour la République) in 1968, and RPR (Rassemblement pour la République) in 1976

Chronology

1890
22 November   De Gaulle born at Lille

1909
27 November   Enters the French military academy of Saint-Cyr

1916
2 March   Wounded at Douaumont: taken prisoner

1921
6 April   Marries Yvonne Vendroux

1924
March   Publication of *La discorde chez l'ennemi*

1925
1 July   Recruited to the general staff of Marshal Pétain

1927
April   Delivers three lectures at the Ecole supérieure de la guerre
25 September   Promoted to the rank of major; sent to Germany as commander of battalion of light infantry in Trier

1929
October   Posted to army of the Levant in Lebanon

1931

November   Return from Lebanon; appointed to General Secre-
                         tariat of National Defence

1932   Publication of *Le fil de l'épée*

1934

May   Publication of *Vers l'armée de métier*
5 December   First meeting with Paul Reynaud

1937

13 July   Appointed to command of 507th tank regiment at
                         Metz

1938

September   Publication of *La France et son armée*

1939

2 September   Appointed commander of tanks in 5th army at
                         Wangenbourg (Alsace)
3 September   Outbreak of Second World War

1940

10 May   German invasion of France
6 June   De Gaulle appointed Under-Secretary of State at the
                         Ministry of War in Reynaud's cabinet
16 June   Reynaud resigns; Pétain becomes Prime Minister
17 June   De Gaulle leaves Bordeaux for London
18 June   Broadcasts 'appel' on the BBC
22 June   France signs armistice
23 June   British government recognizes French National
                         Committee (Free French) in London
28 June   British government recognizes de Gaulle as leader
                         of the Free French
3 July   Destruction of French fleet at Mers-el-Kebir
10 July   Chamber of Deputies votes full powers to Pétain
2 August   De Gaulle condemned to death in his absence
23–6 September   Failure to capture Dakar

1941

22 June   Operation Barbarossa: Germany invades Russia
24 September   Establishment of French National Committee (CNF)
7 December   Pearl Harbour: the USA joins the war

1942

8 November	Operation Torch: allied landings in Algeria
10 November	Admiral Darlan installed as provisional head of government
24 December	Darlan assassinated; General Giraud replaces him

1943

27 May	Founding of the Conseil National de la Résistance (CNR)
30 May	De Gaulle arrives in Algiers from London
3 June	Creation of the French Committee for National Liberation (CFLN) in Algiers

1944

30 January	Brazzaville conference on future of French colonial Africa
3 June	CFLN becomes the provisional government of France (GPRF)
6 June	D-Day: Normandy landings
14 June	De Gaulle returns to France
26 August	Return to Paris: procession down the Champs Elysées

1945

8 May	Surrender of Germany
21 October	Referendum rejects return of Third Republic; election of Constituent Assembly
13 November	De Gaulle unanimously elected president of the provisional government

1946

20 January	De Gaulle resigns from government
16 June	Bayeux speech: de Gaulle's ideas on constitutional change
13 October	Constitution of Fourth Republic endorsed in referendum by 9.2 million votes (8.1 million against and 8.4 million abstentions)

1947

7 April	De Gaulle's speech at Strasbourg launches the Rassemblement du Peuple Français (RPF)
4 May	Ramadier removes communist ministers from government: end of tripartism

19 and 26 October	RPF gets 40 per cent votes in municipal elections
27 October	De Gaulle calls for dissolution of National Assembly
November–December	Widespread strikes

1948

25 February	Prague coup

1949

20 and 27 March	RPF gains 31 per cent vote in cantonal elections
4 April	France signs Atlantic Pact which creates NATO

1950

25 June	Beginning of Korean war

1951

17 June	RPF gains 118 seats out of 625 in elections to Chamber of Deputies

1952

6 March	Antoine Pinay elected prime minister, with help of 27 RPF votes
27 May	France signs treaty founding the European Defence Community

1953

6 May	De Gaulle dissolves the RPF

1954

7 May	Fall of Dien Bien Phu: defeat of French Army in Indochina
18 June	Pierre Mendès-France elected prime minister
20 July	Geneva accords end French rule in Indochina
30 August	Chamber of Deputies rejects the European Defence Community
October	Publication of vol.1 of *Mémoires de guerre*
1 November	Beginning of the Algerian war

1955

6 February	Mendès-France voted out of office
25 February	Edgar Faure becomes prime minister
2 April	State of emergency declared in Algeria
29 November	Faure's government defeated
2 December	Chamber of Deputies dissolved: general election called

1956

2 January	General election
30 January	Guy Mollet becomes prime minister
6 February	Mollet badly received in Algiers: the 'day of tomatoes'.
June	Publication of vol.2 of *Mémoires de guerre*

1957

January–September	'Battle of Algiers'
21 May	Mollet's ministry falls
12 June	Bourgès-Maunoury becomes Prime Minister
15 September	Completion of 'ligne Morice' on Algerian–Tunisian border
30 September	Bourgès-Maunoury's ministry falls
5 November	Gaillard becomes prime minister

1958

8 February	French planes bomb Tunisian village of Sakhiet Sidi Youssef
17 February	France and Tunisia accept US and British conciliation
15 April	Gaillard ministry falls
13 May	Pierre Pflimlin presents ministry to Chamber of Deputies; insurrection in Algiers and formation of Committee of Public Safety
15 May	De Gaulle declares that he is ready to 'take over the powers of the Republic'
19 May	De Gaulle holds press conference
26 May	Evening meeting between de Gaulle and Pflimlin at Saint-Cloud
28 May	Resignation of Pflimlin
29 May	President Coty calls on de Gaulle to take over power
1 June	National Assembly votes in de Gaulle's government by 329 votes to 224
4 June	De Gaulle in Algiers: 'Je vous ai compris'
28 September	Referendum endorses constitution for the Fifth Republic
1 October	Formation of the Union pour la Nouvelle République (UNR)
23 and 30 November	Elections to the Chamber of Deputies: UNR gains 198 seats
21 December	De Gaulle elected President of the Republic

1959

8 January	Formation of the cabinet of Michel Debré
16 September	De Gaulle promises self-determination for Algerians
October	Publication of vol.3 of *Mémoires de guerre*

1960

24 January – 1 February	Week of the barricades in Algeria
29 January	De Gaulle denounces 'week of the barricades'
13 February	Explosion of France's first atomic bomb

1961

8 January	Referendum approves principle of self-determination for Algeria
April	Organisation de l'Armée Secrète (OAS) launches terrorist campaign
22 April	Generals' *putsch* in Algiers
23 April	De Gaulle TV broadcast denounces *putsch* and uses article 16 to assume emergency powers
25 April	*Putsch* collapses
20 May	Negotiations with FLN begin at Evian

1962

18 March	Signing of Evian Accords
8 April	Referendum approves Evian accords
14 April	Resignation of Michel Debré; Georges Pompidou forms new ministry
15 May	De Gaulle derides European integration and dangers of 'volapük'; resignation of MRP ministers
1 July	Referendum on Algerian independence
22 July	Assassination attempt fails at Petit-Clamart
5 October	Motion of censure passed against Pompidou's ministry
10 October	Chamber of Deputies dissolved: new elections called
28 October	Referendum accepts election of President by universal suffrage
18–25 November	Elections to Chamber of Deputies give UNR 233 seats; with support of other parties, now has majority of 285 seats

1963

22 January	Franco-German treaty of co-operation
14 January	De Gaulle rejects United Kingdom application for membership of EEC
1 March	Beginning of miners' strike

1964
27 January   France recognizes Communist China

1965
1 July   France withdraws from Council of Ministers of EEC
                     in protest against Hallstein plan
10 September   FGDS founded by the Socialist and Radical Parties,
                     and the clubs of the Convention des Institutions
                     Républicaines (CIR)
5 and 19 December   De Gaulle defeats François Mitterrand in presiden-
                     tial election, on the second round

1966
8 January   Pompidou forms his third ministry
7 March   French forces withdrawn from NATO
1 September   De Gaulle begins state visit to Cambodia
21 December   Agreement between FGDS and PCF to co-ordinate
                     votes in forthcoming election

1967
5 and 12 March   Elections to Chamber of Deputies; UNR reduced to
                     200 seats; FGDS and PCF gain
1 and 4 April   Pompidou forms fourth ministry
16 May   De Gaulle states opposition to second attempt of the
                     UK to join EEC
6 June   Beginning of the 'Six Day War' between Israel and
                     Arab states
16 June   Chamber authorizes government to take economic
                     and social decisions by decree
23–27 July   De Gaulle visits Canada: 'Vive le Québec libre'
27 November   De Gaulle criticizes Israel as 'an élite people, sure
                     of itself and dominating...'

1968
3 May   Sorbonne cleared by police
10–11 May   'Night of the barricades' in the Latin Quarter of Paris
11 May   Pompidou returns from state visit to Afghanistan;
                     Sorbonne reopened
13 May   24-hour strike: workers and students march against
                     police brutality
14–18 May   De Gaulle on state visit to Romania; general strike
                     develops
24 May   De Gaulle broadcasts on radio and television with
                     promise of referendum on university reform and
                     'participation'

24–5 May	Serious riots in many cities
25 May	Grenelle negotiations with unions start
27 May	Grenelle accords rejected by workers at Renault plant at Billancourt
27 May	Mass meeting at the Charléty stadium in Paris
28 May	François Mitterrand states he will be presidential candidate if de Gaulle steps down; Mendès-France to be his prime minister
29 May	De Gaulle's helicopter ride to Baden-Baden and Massu
30 May	Radio broadcast announces dissolution of National Assembly and general election; Gaullist demonstration on the Champs-Elysées
31 May	Pompidou forms fifth cabinet
23–30 June	UNR sweeps home in general election
10 July	Pompidou resigns
12 July	Couve de Murville forms new ministry
20–21 July	Soviet Union imposes military occupation of Czechoslovakia

1969

17 January	Pompidou states his intention of being candidate for presidency if de Gaulle retires
27 April	Referendum on regional reorganization and reform of Senate: de Gaulle's proposals defeated
28 April	De Gaulle resigns as president
15 June	Pompidou elected his successor
29 May–18 June	De Gaulle's private visit to Ireland

1970

3–21 June	Holiday in Spain
October 1970	Publication of *Mémoires d'espoir, Vol.1: Le Renouveau, 1958–62*
9 November	De Gaulle dies at Colombey-les-Deux-Eglises

Introduction

Hugh Gough and John Horne

In the years since de Gaulle's death in 1970, studies of his life and various aspects of his politics have proliferated. This book, however, is neither biography nor monograph. Rather, it is a series of explorations of de Gaulle's political career and of its connections with the evolution of France during the thirty dramatic years which it spanned, from 1940 to 1969. Adopting an essentially thematic approach, the volume looks in two directions, towards mid-twentieth-century France as well as towards the source and substance of de Gaulle's politics, and aims to provide the reader with a basis for assessing the historical significance of de Gaulle as politician and statesman.

The book has a further particularity in that it brings together contributions by leading French as well as anglophone experts on de Gaulle. It thus provides a rare opportunity for an anglophone public to read historians whose thoughts on de Gaulle have not been easily accessible in English. By the same token, it succinctly presents the reader with a wide spectrum of views on de Gaulle and poses the question of where the balance of opinion on his significance now lies.

The ways in which de Gaulle entered and left politics are revealing about the public persona and historical role of the man. Each was framed by a dramatic statement – the radio broadcast on the BBC on 18 June 1940 and the press communiqué issued on 27 April 1969. Throughout his public career, words were to be the indispensable political medium for a man whose genius lay in understanding not only the underlying dramas of history but also the theatricality of politics. But the nature of those opening and closing declarations also reveals two contrasting political roles – characterized by Jean Lacouture in his masterly biography as the rebel and the ruler. De Gaulle entered politics in 1940 as the military rebel, a lone general who defied the armistice policy adopted by the Pétain government at Bordeaux and proclaimed instead continuing national resistance, despite the crushing defeat inflicted on France by Germany. He left politics as the defeated ruler, abiding by the political structures which he himself had placed at the heart of his 1958 constitution for the new, Fifth Republic, and which had denied him victory in the referendum through which he sought to renew his legitimacy after the sudden upheaval of May 1968. The connections between the rebel and the ruler form a major theme of this volume.

In reality, the rebel had already emerged in a minor key before the trauma of May–June 1940. Not far short of fifty when the Second World War broke out, de Gaulle had written a series of works on military matters which marked him as unconventional – by the breadth of his political and diplomatic understanding as much as by his advocacy of mechanized warfare and his uncompromising repudiation of appeasement. None the less, de Gaulle, like Pétain, remained essentially a military figure who would not have found a political role without the dislocation caused by national defeat. Both men, and they were personally linked in complex and ironic ways, responded politically to military catastrophe, as René Rémond shows in the opening essay. But where the aged marshal and hero of Verdun masked military abdication with the belief that political accommodation with the Germans was possible, the better to turn his energies to purging France of those held responsible for national defeat, de Gaulle took the quixotic step of proclaiming that the independence of the French state, and implicitly the place of France in the first rank of nations, were the indispensable conditions for national survival, conditions which could only be guaranteed by a refusal to accept German victory as definitive. 'We are France', de Gaulle remarked of the Free French. His call to resistance in 1940 constituted what François Bédarida, in his essay, describes as the fundamental 'legitimizing event' of his political career, and the source and nature of de Gaulle's political legitimacy form a second major theme of this volume.

To the extent that the French for the next quarter century, if not longer, were haunted by the débâcle of 1940, de Gaulle's incarnation of undefeated independence in the nation's darkest moment remained at the heart of his subsequent political appeal. Conversely, de Gaulle derived from the humiliation of 1940 the conviction that the strength and independence of the state must constitute the core of national politics. The symbiotic but at times troubled relationship between these two aspects of the legitimizing moment of 1940 marked de Gaulle's entire public career. The popular legitimacy ensured by his stand in 1940, and his subsequent skill in playing a weak political hand against the allies, led directly to the apotheosis of 26 August 1944 when de Gaulle walked through the cheering crowds of liberated Paris and presided as head of the provisional government over post-war political reconstruction down to January 1946. It was ultimately this same 'legitimizing event' of 1940 which nearly twenty years later endowed de Gaulle with the necessary authority to resolve the Algerian crisis.

Yet de Gaulle always sought to translate this legitimacy into policies which would tangibly strengthen the state, and therefore France. In particular he asserted a distinct French identity and autonomy in international affairs and, even more fundamentally, tried to recast domestic political institutions in order to strengthen executive authority, which remained notoriously weak in the republican parliamentary tradition. De Gaulle's foreign policy – the Algerian question aside – received considerable support from French opinion despite (or perhaps because of) its capacity to exasperate France's friends and allies. As Douglas Johnson shows, it was precisely those features which might appear anachronistic or illusory abroad – his prickly independence with relation to America, the nuclear deterrent, the concept of a Europe free from super-power hegemony – which rallied consensus at home through their reassuring suggestion that France had recovered something of the *grandeur* (greatness) lost in the Second World War.

Refashioning the constitution was a different and far more contentious matter. De Gaulle resigned over the impossibility of achieving it in January 1946, passing into the wilderness years of the Fourth Republic. When called on to resolve the Algerian crisis in 1958, however, he used what amounted to a renewal of legitimacy, won through painfully confronting the French with the inevitability of decolonization, in order to pursue his underlying purpose of constitutional reform. Michel Winock argues that de Gaulle himself did not envisage the ultimate solution of complete independence for Algeria when he returned to power (as he later claimed in his memoirs). The events of 1960 – from the week of the barricades in Algiers to the collapse of the newly established French Community of former African colonies – played the crucial role in convincing de Gaulle that his alternative strategy of a Franco-Algerian 'association' was impracticable. From then on, the acceptance of some form of independence was only a question of timing and negotiation. But from the start, de Gaulle was pragmatic in his attitude to the status of Algeria, subordinating it to his over-riding concern with restoring French strength and independence. Above all, as Michel Winock argues, the originality of de Gaulle was to use the successive stages of the resolution of the crisis to restructure the political institutions of France in favour of a strong presidency, through the constitution of the new Fifth Republic (September 1958) and the addition of direct presidential elections in 1962.

A fourth theme raised by many of the contributions to this book is the relationship between the political mystique generated by de Gaulle's role as man of 'destiny' and French politics in a more conventional and routine sense. De Gaulle's understanding of politics was stamped by long-standing military concerns with authority, leadership and strategy. Together with the extraordinary circumstances which twice brought him to power, this helps explain his Olympian aloofness from the cut and thrust of day-to-day politics. De Gaulle considered himself a repository of national integrity and the authority of the state, the incarnation of 'a certain idea of France' which encompassed all the historic divisions and ideological currents of the nation while aligning him with none of them. In conventional terms he saw himself as a man of neither right nor left. Being thus in some sense above 'politics', de Gaulle could act as a centre and symbol of *rassemblement* (national unity), most notably during the Second World War.

But the Gaullist mystique could scarcely avoid some embroilment in low politics. Already during the war, as François Bédarida notes, de Gaulle had an uneasy relationship with the internal resistance until the final 'parting of the ways' in autumn 1944, and there was a Resistance myth of the French war effort which paralleled the Gaullist myth. It was not ideological diversity which subverted de Gaulle's conception of politics, however, but sectional conflict and the 'regime of political parties'. Revulsion at the re-emergence of traditional parliamentary politics prompted his resignation in January 1946 and fifteen months later led him to launch his new political formation, the Rassemblement du Peuple Français, to campaign against the constitution of the newly established Fourth Republic. But turning Gaullism into a political movement failed to inspire the *rassemblement* on which de Gaulle's legitimacy was premised, so long as 'destiny' declined to intervene in the form of a crisis of the regime. Worse, it risked compromising Gaullist mystique in the political marketplace. Yet as Jean-Pierre Rioux explains, this neglected period of de Gaulle's career, during the Fourth Republic of 1946 to 1958, is deeply instructive about de Gaulle's approach to politics. By 1953, de Gaulle had abandoned the experiment of mobilizing his legitimacy through a political movement. Instead, he took refuge in the word, writing his *War Memoirs* (1954–9) in order to reconstruct the founding mythology of the war years while waiting for the providential circumstances in which it might be politically reactivated. Robert Pickering demonstrates, moreover, that here as elsewhere there was no contradiction for de Gaulle between word and action. Both were linked in a creative dynamic that structures the entire text of the *War Memoirs*, producing a modern epic.

The resolution of the tension between mystique and movement, between the high politics of national destiny and the low politics of the 'regime of parties', came, of course, with the crisis of 1958 which allowed de Gaulle to act as the indispensable figure of national *rassemblement* while devising a constitutional form for his political vision. The formation of a Gaullist party in 1958 was a consequence, not a cause, of the Gaullist republic, and support for Gaullism was, and has remained, a much narrower phenomenon than approval for de Gaulle himself and his political institutions, as Serge Berstein's contribution reminds us. With its strong presidential authority (exercised by de Gaulle in defence and foreign affairs) and a mandate and term of office sharply distinguishing the presidency from parliament, the constitution of the Fifth Republic enshrines de Gaulle's conception of a powerful executive above the divisiveness of daily politics without, for all that, abolishing the 'regime of parties'. For Serge Berstein, this amounts to a 'new republican model' which replaced the outmoded one created in the late nineteenth century under the Third Republic, and which won the support of the new social groups emerging with the economic and social transformations of post-war France. In this view, de Gaulle's achievement was not just to build a constitution around his own concept of political leadership but also to provide a constitutional framework which facilitated political stability at a time of rapid social change.

All this makes the third crisis of de Gaulle's political career, that of May 1968, the most enigmatic. Julian Jackson's detailed reconstruction of de Gaulle's response to the 'Events' shows a man caught off guard by an upheaval which defied conventional criteria. Neither involving factious parties nor targeting the institutions of state, the amorphous movement of discontented students and then striking workers swelled from the depths of a society which it brought to a standstill, without ever crystallizing a political challenge to the regime. Whether a symptom of the malaise provoked by post-war social change or a youthful rejection of the paternalist and authoritarian style of Gaullist politics, the May Events shook de Gaulle profoundly. Seizing the initiative in almost military fashion by his sudden disappearance to Germany and dramatic return to a radio broadcast which evoked the memories of his wartime past, his rhetoric worked its magic one last time. But the Gaullist triumph in the subsequent general election rang hollow for de Gaulle. May 1968 challenged de Gaulle's own sense of his legitimacy and dissolved the working relationship between de Gaulle's mystique and Gaullist politics. Failing to rehabilitate his legitimacy in the 1969 referendum on an issue which it had never encompassed – regional reform and decentralization of the state – de Gaulle left the stage to the Gaullist politicians, notably Pompidou, who had been the real victors in May 1968.

One final theme is raised by almost all the contributions – the style and personal motivation of de Gaulle's politics. De Gaulle's disdain for the politics of faction and division implied no reluctance to pursue his own goals ruthlessly. A subtle tactician as well as a dominant personality, legendary in his personal abrasiveness while able to command the

deepest loyalty, de Gaulle generated opposed views of his political morality – from man of undeviating principle to calculating machiavellian.
As a politician, de Gaulle was tactically extremely versatile, yet his aims
were governed by the vision that he had for France and for her role in
the world which he pursued single-mindedly. But that abiding concern
for France, as Jean-Marie Mayeur shows, coexisted with sincere religious
faith. This never conflicted with his perception of politics as a secular
activity and of the state as independent within its own sphere. He accepted the autonomy of the political world and allied himself with the
tradition of Richelieu rather than that of Louis XIV or Charles X. Yet in
many ways de Gaulle's Catholicism shaped the deep sense of morality
which informed his political, no less than his personal, decisions.

Taken together, the contributions to this volume bear ample testimony
to the continued historical significance of de Gaulle. This is due in good
measure to his reputation as the embodiment of national unity during
the war. In the opening paragraph of his contribution, François Bédarida
cites the SOFRES opinion poll of November 1990 in which half of those
questioned remembered de Gaulle primarily as the man of the resistance
in 1940. However the significance of his resistance role was undoubtedly
magnified by his political achievements between 1958 and 1969 in
extricating France from a bitter colonial entanglement and creating a new
set of political institutions. Only the future will tell whether de Gaulle's
constitution has provided a definitive synthesis of authority and representation for the French. But it stands as the second longest-lasting
regime since 1789, with one of its fiercest initial opponents, François
Mitterrand, as its longest-serving president, and it commands unprecedented consensus among the modern-day French. As Julian Jackson
observes, de Gaulle is now benefiting – as he himself predicted shortly
before his death – from retrospective apotheosis through the growth of
his own myth. He has become part of the national patrimony, one of
those *lieux de mémoire* which underpin the collective memory of the
French, a figure of consensus around which various political viewpoints
can gather to reinforce their own legitimacy.

There is a certain irony in all this, for de Gaulle himself was never a
man of consensus. His political career was marked instead by conflict,
by a stubborn defence of his own political principles against colleagues
and opponents, and by an individualism which rejected the strictures
of political parties. The constitution of the Fifth Republic was bitterly
contested at its inception as a neo-Bonapartist charter, a licence for
authoritarianism. It is almost as if the passage of time has softened the
sharp edges of de Gaulle's abrasive personality, cast a veil over the
frequently partisan nature of his political activity, and moulded him into
a monument which all can admire, because different angles of vision
reveal different shapes of the man. Time has undoubtedly been kind to

his memory, and this may in part be due to the waning strength of Gaullism and its continued separation from the mystique of de Gaulle himself. But it is also a measure of de Gaulle's real achievements in resolving the colonial and constitutional blocks to France's development and in helping to create a more self-confident and outward-looking country. Above all, perhaps, de Gaulle's personal legitimacy endorsed a set of values, and provided a series of self-images, which have helped the French in the long work of coming to terms with the trauma of the war years. In these ways, and more, de Gaulle's legacy remains central to an understanding of modern France.

1

Two Destinies: Pétain and de Gaulle

René Rémond

It might be asked at the outset whether there is any justification other than rhetorical for the subject of this essay. It is true that in France biography as a genre has recovered a legitimacy long denied it, and has found renewed favour with historians. For this we are indebted to the masterpiece that is Jean Lacouture's biography of Charles de Gaulle, as well as to several studies of Philippe Pétain.[1] But what considerations could lead us to deal with these two historical figures on the model of Plutarch's parallel *Lives*? To this objection concerning the substance of my title might be added another which is all the more forceful in the present context. For it might seem provocative to link these two historical personalities in a volume whose *raison d'être* is the evocation of the first *résistant*, and to compare de Gaulle with a man, Pétain, whose name remains forever linked with the signing of the armistice. It must be admitted that very sound reasons would be required to overcome these two objections.

Such reasons certainly exist, however, and their enunciation will serve as the connecting link in what follows, proceeding from the most individual and contingent of them to the most general and essential – that is, to those linked to the destiny of France as a whole, as it was reflected in each of these two individual destinies. We must certainly look at what connected the two men, and at the analogies between them, but we must also look at the irreducible differences between them both at the level of

---

[1] J. Lacouture, *De Gaulle* , Vol. 1, *The Rebel, 1890–1944* (Collins–Harvill, London, 1990); Vol. 2, *The Ruler, 1945–1970* (Collins–Harvill, London, 1991); H. Lottman, *Pétain, Hero or Traitor: the Untold Story* (Viking, London, 1985); M. Ferro, *Pétain* (Fayard, Paris, 1987); G. Pedroncini, *Pétain, le soldat de la gloire 1856–1918* (Perrin, Paris, 1989).

objective reality and of the symbolic world, which has such importance for the memory of a people.

The chance encounters between the two men come most naturally to mind. In spite of belonging to the same institution, namely the army, they might easily never have met prior to clashing in 1940. Indeed, they were more likely not to have come to know each other than the reverse, if only because of their great difference in age. Thirty-four years, almost the span of an army career, separated their respective graduations from the military academy of Saint-Cyr. Pétain was ready to retire as colonel when the young Charles de Gaulle received his first posting. Born during the Second Empire, Pétain was fourteen in 1870, old enough to have witnessed and retained a memory of his country's defeat. De Gaulle, on the other hand, was born twenty years later and had merely heard tell of it. He reached the age of fourteen at the time of the first Moroccan crisis of 1905.

It was the accident of military postings which brought the two men face to face. The facts are well-known and have been minutely established by historians. Raymond Tournoux has devoted a whole book to the relationship between Pétain and de Gaulle.[2] I shall therefore limit myself to recalling briefly circumstances which in themselves were minor, but which assume great historical significance when they concern personalities of such magnitude. At that time, students admitted to the military academy had to begin by spending a year in a military formation. Charles de Gaulle did this in his home region, the department of the Nord, in the 33rd Infantry Regiment at Arras. On graduating from the academy, he quite naturally asked to return to this regiment, whose colonel since October 1912 had been Philippe Pétain. Thus the young second lieutenant began his career and served his apprenticeship in military command under the orders of the future marshal. We know from his writings that the young officer held his superior in high regard, admiring his professional qualities and his touchy sense of independence. The colonel, for his part, gave his junior officer highly laudatory reports. Such was the first episode in the history of the relationship between the two men, which lasted just over a year. Pétain left the 33rd to take command of a brigade, and their ways parted. During the First World War, Pétain rapidly ascended all the rungs of the military hierarchy, finishing the war crowned with glory as the hero of Verdun and with a marshal's baton. He had become, to use the felicitous expression of Jean Lacouture, the 'Imperator'.

The two men were to meet again in 1925, when Pétain appointed de Gaulle to his staff. It seems that de Gaulle owed this mark of attention

[2] J. R. Tournoux, *Pétain and de Gaulle* (1964; English translation: Heinemann, London, 1966).

mainly to his talent as a writer, revealed a year earlier with the publication of *La Discorde chez l' ennemi*. Pétain had literary ambitions and needed the presence at his side of what Lacouture elegantly calls 'an officer of the pen'. It was also a question of writing which sowed discord between them ten years later. Pétain intervened repeatedly in de Gaulle's career, raising the latter's marks on his graduation from the Ecole Supérieure de Guerre (staff college), and going so far as to impose him on the school as a lecturer in 1927. This episode is well-known, with Pétain himself introducing the lecturer in the most flattering terms which were bound to excite the jealousy of de Gaulle's comrades. The relationship between the illustrious marshal and the young officer with a promising future were at this point close, almost affectionate. De Gaulle dedicated his writings to Pétain, a fact which would be frequently remarked on subsequently, and which was responsible for a persistent rumour during the Second World War that Pétain was godfather to de Gaulle's son, also named Philippe. Public opinion would take this as the sign of an unspoken agreement, even of a concerted effort, by the two men to share roles in the face of the enemy. The relationship between Pétain and de Gaulle also had a resonant human dimension, with all the elements of a classical drama – no longer Plutarch but a Greek tragedy. These were not strangers who would confront each other in the future, but men whose lives and careers were intimately linked.

The relationship was to grow colder and more distant. Pétain grew disappointed in his expectations, de Gaulle wounded in his pride. It is doubtful whether any disagreement relating to strategic options played a part in this progressive estrangement. The rupture occurred when de Gaulle reasserted his freedom and took back the manuscript of a book which he had ghost-written for Pétain (but which the latter had not published), publishing it under his own name as *La France et son armée*, in 1938. From this date, the two men did not meet again until the dark days of 1940, in cabinet meetings moving from château to château ahead of the enemy advance. Pétain had been Deputy Prime Minister since mid-May 1940 and de Gaulle was appointed Under-Secretary of State for Defence on 6 June. They thus overlapped in government for little more than ten days, though each one counted for many ordinary days. Their last meeting took place in Bordeaux. They never saw each other again, all further contact being on the world stage as they challenged each other rhetorically and fought each other from a distance. Henceforth, their history was no longer a matter of personal destiny, but of what they personified, of the antithetical choices signified by their names, of the causes with which they were identified.

The sixteenth of June 1940 marked the parting of their ways. Pétain called for an armistice, claiming responsibility for its immediate and long-term consequences, and declaring with some haughtiness, in the aftermath of the Montoire meeting: 'History will be my judge'. De Gaulle immediately condemned this option, refusing to accept that the war was over, denouncing the undertakings of 'governments of circumstance', and calling on the French people to continue fighting. The antagonism between the two men and their political options would keep growing. Free French radio broadcasts gradually became more severe towards the Marshal, running the risk of shocking those for whom he still commanded veneration and admiration, even if they did not approve of all his initiatives. Vichy condemned all dissidents and pursued without pity all those it suspected of Gaullism. The confrontation became irrevocable. In the summer of 1940, a court martial formed by the Vichy government sentenced the head of state's former protégé to death in his absence. Five years later, in the summer of 1945, the High Court, formed at the instigation of the Provisional Government, in turn condemned Marshal Pétain to death. What could be more dramatic than this singular battle between two protagonists who had for so long lived in close familiarity with each other and who now mutually condemned each other to death. Would Pétain have carried out the death sentence if de Gaulle had fallen into Vichy's hands? It seems to have been out of the question, just as de Gaulle commuted Pétain's own death sentence to life imprisonment. The rule of symmetry was respected.

If we enter into a somewhat deeper comparison of the two men's destinies, the similarities between them are numerous, starting with their attitudes to war. This is hardly surprising, when we consider the part that war played in the lives of their respective generations – war experienced, prepared for, expected or more generally feared, war endured. War completely overturned their existence and the course of their lives. Without it Pétain would have retired and de Gaulle would probably have had a more brilliant career, reaching a higher rank than that of temporary general of a brigade. But without war, neither of them would have occupied a place in historical memory. It was war and the fortunes of war which rescued them from obscurity, made them figures of the first importance and even notoriety. Both men first knew glory (in the fullest sense of the term) through war. Both men could be said to have been the most illustrious Frenchmen of their times. Pétain enjoyed the more complete and undeniable military fame. In 1940, his prestige was unequalled, a whole nation revered him, and thousands of his former soldiers from the First World War were eternally grateful to him for having spared their blood. These feelings were the foundation of the myth of Pétain and formed the basis of his immense authority. As for de Gaulle, President Coty, welcoming him to the Elysée Palace in January 1959, remarked felicitously that 'the first among Frenchmen is from now on the first man of France'. The conqueror of Verdun, the first resister: such a parallel alone would justify this essay.

It was also war which turned these soldiers into political figures. The first phase of the Second World War, marked by apparent defeat, had a contrasting impact on each of them. Defeat brought Pétain to supreme power, since from 10 July 1940 the full powers of the National Assembly, and more, were placed in his hands. He arrogated to himself the power of judgement when he decided to intern without sentence the politicians whom he held responsible for the defeat. The entire French people placed themselves in his hands as the saviour of the defeated nation. De Gaulle, on the other hand, stood almost alone, but he too acted as a political figure. His genius lay in presenting himself not as a soldier leading a small band of men into battle, but as a political leader purporting to raise up the abandoned state and symbolically to represent France.

Comparing the consequences of wartime for the two men extends beyond the Second World War. If the defeat of the French Army in 1940 brought Pétain to power, the drawn-out war in Algeria brought de Gaulle back to power in 1958. Of course, the two situations and conflicts are not exactly comparable. The undeclared war in Algeria set the French Army against a nationalist insurrection in a territory which, legally and historically, was under French sovereignty. Furthermore, the Front de Libération Nationale (FLN) was never in a position to inflict defeat on the French Army on its own ground – in sharp contrast to the case of Indochina. Yet there are undoubted analogies between the political consequences of the Algerian War and the Battle of France in 1940. The latter brought about the fall of the Third Republic and ensured Pétain's accession to power just as the Fourth Republic's failure to find either a military or a diplomatic solution to the Algerian problem brought about its constitutional downfall and led to the return of de Gaulle.

There are also similarities in the processes of transition from one regime to another. In both cases, the transfer of power was effected, or covered, by means of an Act of Parliament maintaining the appearances of legality. There was no *coup* or seizure of power. On 10 July 1940 and 1 June 1958, a parliamentary majority (stronger in the first case) pronounced itself in favour of change. Similarities should not, of course, obscure the profound differences between the two situations, notably the fact that in 1940, France was partially occupied by a conquering enemy. But the resemblance between them has been noted by many and played a part in the decision of those who refused to vote in favour of General de Gaulle in 1958. The memory of the capitulation of parliament and the example of the eighty members who refused to grant full powers to Pétain may well have been factors in determining the attitude of a Pierre Mendès-France or a François Mitterrand, who turned against de Gaulle the lesson they had learned from him on 18 June 1940. Rather than the immediate circumstances of 1958, it was the subsequent nature of the new regime which gave the lie to the idea of any more substantial similarity between Vichy and the Fifth Republic.

None the less, it remains the case that the majority of public opinion and a large proportion of the political élite, faced with two exceptional situations eighteen years apart, drew the same conclusion – that the regime had collapsed. The institutions which had been responsible for defeat and failure therefore had to be changed. Pétain and de Gaulle were each in turn handed power by parliament and given a mandate to prepare a new constitution. In neither case was this power unconditional, the setting up of a new regime being subject to certain conditions. On 10 July 1940, all powers were given to the 'government of the Republic' (it is worth noting the use of this term as a guarantee that the republican form would not be abandoned) 'under the authority and signature of Marshal Pétain'. The text also provided for ratification of the new constitution by the nation, though circumstances prevented this taking place. On 3 June 1958, the government received a mandate to prepare a new constitution. This initiative took place within a framework of firm guidelines. The memory of 10 July 1940 was undoubtedly determinant in the application of these precautionary measures.

The analogy between these two processes of transition can be extended to a clear affinity of inspiration behind the institutional practices of the two regimes. The common objective was to put an end to the omnipotence of parliament by restoring the balance of power, disrupted since the conclusion of the crisis of 16 May 1877 to the detriment of the executive. Both constitutional projects rejected the idea that national sovereignty should rest exclusively with parliamentary representation. The parallel between the two cases should not be pushed too far, not only because Vichy's constitutional projects remained on the drawing board, whereas the French have now lived for a third of a century under the constitution of 1958 inspired by de Gaulle, but even more because, from common premises, the intentions and practices have fundamentally diverged. Vichy showed itself to be reactionary in the proper sense of the term, systematically opposing the principles of 1789, whereas the evolution of the Fifth Republic has refuted those who feared for democracy in 1958, achieving important advances in the democratization of French institutions and political life.

Before returning to this divergence, one last point of comparison between these individual destinies must be suggested – the notion of their complementarity in the years 1940–4. This was a widespread idea at the time, and it is one which still finds supporters today among certain defenders of the memory of Marshal Pétain. According to this view, Pétain and de Gaulle divided wartime roles or, if they did not do so explicitly through a concerted effort, at any rate their actions were parallel. This theory has been formulated and worked out through images which have become classic: the shield which Pétain is supposed to have interposed between Germany and France, the sword taken up by de

Gaulle and the image, too, used by Colonel Rémy, of the two strings which France was fortunate enough to have to her bow. At the time numerous French people believed, or wanted to believe, in the existence of a secret agreement between the two men. The personal relationship between them lent some credence to this interpretation. Others hoped this was the case without really believing it. It is an idea which still finds its advocates, and is implicit in a recent book on the period by François-Georges Dreyfus.[3] But it is a view which is no longer tenable. Neither Pétain nor de Gaulle ever expressed their approval of this interpretation of history – indeed, they even refuted it. Pétain felt that dissidence weakened his authority in the face of German demands. The legitimacy of his government was founded on an obsession with the theme of rallying the country around his own person, and he appealed to the French to unite in emotional terms which scarcely lent themselves to a strategy based on duplicity. He passionately denounced division and the Vichy police ruthlessly hunted down Gaullists. As for de Gaulle, he never tired of repeating that the Vichy government was misleading the French by making them believe in the possibility of an agreement with the victor and that it was leading the country into a ruinous ambiguity. Moreover, he disclaimed Rémy's theory of the two strings to France's bow.

But in the absence of personal support by either man for the thesis of convergence between Vichy and the Free French, it might still be argued that there was an objective complementarity between the two. It is here that we need to extend the comparison of individual destinies definitively beyond the personal dimension in order to consider what these two historical figures symbolized, what their choices meant for their followers, and more generally, since both gave their names to political currents as well as to historical periods, the ideas to which their names have been linked, namely *pétainisme* and *gaullisme*.

In fact, the difference between Pétain and de Gaulle, *pétainisme* and *gaullisme*, is both profound and irreducible. Their disagreement in 1940 had its roots in the divergence that existed between two conceptions of politics whose inspirations and foundations were incompatible. Their respective political philosophies stood in total opposition to each other. Vichy was counter-revolutionary, with Pétain's National Revolution systematically opposed to the principles of 1789 that had given birth to modern French society. It rested on the principle of authority which could only come from above and had nothing but distrust for the right to vote, particularly when this last was made available to all. Its aim was to restore a hierarchical order in society.

Gaullism, both in wartime and in the Fifth Republic, identified itself with the restoration of democracy. Power was legitimate only in so far

[3]F.-G. Dreyfus, *Histoire de Vichy* (Perrin, Paris, 1990).

as it was the expression of universal suffrage. The nation alone was sovereign. De Gaulle promised to give power back to the people and he kept his promise. He chose to let the electors decide on whether to return to the Fourth Republic or to create new institutions by way of referendum. In 1962 he took the power to elect the President of the Republic away from a restricted electoral college and gave it to the totality of the electorate.

Pétainisme and *gaullisme* thus underwent a curious mutual reversal. Pétain, who passed for the most republican of wartime leaders because of his humble origins and because he had not been educated in a religious institution, found himself on the extreme right of the political stage, whereas the aristocratic officer who had grown up in a deeply Catholic family supported democracy and restored the Republic. Their respective doctrines were also related to different perspectives on French history. The National Revolution adhered to a Manichean vision inspired by the philosophy of the counter-revolution, a philosophy which was conveyed and renewed by the Action Française and which excluded whole and essential periods of history for the simple reason that they deviated from the only tradition which this movement associated with France, namely the royalist and religious tradition of the *ancien régime*. This selective interpretation of history was in harmony with a form of nationalism based on exclusion. The Gaullist view of French history, on the other hand, was comprehensive and accepted it in its entirety. It went hand in hand with the ideology of the rallying of the nation, which is the very essence of Gaullism: France is neither the right nor the left, but the two at once.

The fact is that *pétainisme* and *gaullisme* did not refer to the same idea of France, nor did they imply the same definition of the nation. The choice of June 1940 suddenly revealed the divergence of these two conceptions and separated them, setting them one against the other. For Pétain, France was enclosed in a well-defined area, linked by a special bond to the earth and to its landscapes. Far from his natural borders, the French person would lose his roots. This conception of France, in a term dear to the poet Péguy, might be called *charnelle* (corporeal) if the word had not been corrupted from its original significance precisely by the propaganda of Vichy. For de Gaulle and for the Free French, France was wherever French people were fighting for honour and freedom. France was identified with moral and spiritual values and defined by a mission which transcended the circumstances of time or place.

Such is the deep significance of the gesture of 18 June, whose meaning goes beyond the fate that befell France in the summer of 1940. From the depths of the abyss it stated that there is no such thing as historical inevitability, that courage and will-power can change the course of events. It is here, beyond the confrontation between two personalities of the first importance, beyond the conflict between two political figures, that the historical grandeur of the appeal of 18 June lies. The miracle is that history was on the side of the man who did not despair.

2

De Gaulle and the Resistance
1940–1944

François Bédarida

In November 1990, on the centenary of de Gaulle's birth and the twentieth anniversary of his death, a survey carried out by the French opinion poll agency SOFRES showed that as far as the French were concerned, not only was he the single most important figure of French history in the twentieth century (and the second most important, after Napoleon, in the entire history of the nation), but that the dominant feature of his participation in that history was the role that he had played during the Second World War. Foremost in the collective memory of the French nation, in other words, was the man who called for resistance and refused to accept defeat. The answers to one of the questions asked in the survey make this very clear. Given the choice of various possible replies to the question 'What do you remember General de Gaulle for: the appeal of 18 June 1940, the Liberation, the foundation of the Fifth Republic?', etc., 43 per cent of those surveyed cited the appeal of 18 June. The Liberation came second with 26 per cent, followed by foundation of the Fifth Republic with only 15 per cent, the ending of the Algerian War with 7 per cent, and so on.

When it came to naming the high points in de Gaulle's life and works, the appeal of 18 June swept into the lead, with the approval of 84 per cent (roughly level with the introduction in 1962 of presidential elections by universal suffrage) followed by the resistance to Nazism with 75 per cent. However, his refusal to co-operate with Marshal Pétain still met with the approval of 54 per cent of those surveyed, and the inclusion of communist ministers in the post-Liberation government scored 50 per cent. One can see, therefore, the extent to which the collective memory of the French accords priority to actions taken during the war years, years of combat and resistance for the honour of France and for freedom from enemy oppression.

In fact, at a very early stage in his wartime career, the leader of Free France had intended to bring together the internal and external Resistance movements. He later said to Malraux, referring to the Resistance : 'There was no one, apart from them, to carry on the war that began in 1914. Like the men of Bir Hakeim, the men of the Resistance were above all witnesses'.[1] The link between de Gaulle and the Resistance, indissoluble from that moment on, and subsequently bound together as much by myth as by the course of history, is none the less one that requires careful analysis by the historian, if we are to retrace its various stages, discern its constituent parts, distinguish the areas of agreement and conflict, and ultimately, deconstruct its mythologies.

Three main periods of development can be traced between 1940 and 1944. To each of them might be applied the very terms invented by de Gaulle in the threefold division of his war memoirs. The 'call' covers the period from early 1940 until 1942; 'unity' is achieved in the course of 1943, and with 1944 comes 'salvation', or the preparation for the Liberation, followed by the Liberation itself. From autumn 1944 on, a brief but dramatic epilogue is played out – the 'parting of the ways'.

Everything begins with the famous line from the appeal of 18 June: 'Whatever happens, the flame of the French resistance must not, and will not, be quenched'. On close examination, however, within this apparently limpid phrase can be found both a starting point and a discourse that is inherently ambivalent. That it represents a starting point is obvious, since it is from that moment on that de Gaulle's legitimacy was established. It was the starting point of his mission, the source and the symbol of an exceptional and unprecedented national destiny, a destiny that was lived in the name of 'a certain idea of France': the idea that France was eternal, and that this eternal France could not be vanquished, even by the worst defeat in its history.

On this point, there was total agreement with the internal Resistance, for they shared the same basic conviction as de Gaulle: that France was still at war, despite the armistice, and that this war, fought for a just cause, would become a global conflict in which the French should continue to play their part. There were many scattered signs of this conviction. On the day of the armistice itself, Edmond Michelet copied texts by Péguy for distribution in the letter-boxes of his town, Brive-la-Gaillarde, which proclaimed the moral superiority of non-surrender over surrender. On

[1]Quoted by André Malraux in *Fallen Oaks. Conversation with de Gaulle,* translated by Irene Clephane (1971: English translation: Hamish Hamilton, London, 1972), p.112. These words were spoken in 1964 at the opening of the exhibition on the Resistance held at the Invalides on the occasion of the twentieth anniversary of the Liberation and the fiftieth anniversary of the beginning of the First World War.

25 November 1940, in the founding issue of the newspaper *Liberté*, published clandestinely in the free zone, François de Menthon – who would later join forces with Henri Frenay to found the *Combat* movement – wrote: 'We refuse to admit defeat. We refuse even more emphatically to help Germany conquer us permanently. We can contribute to Germany's defeat, and for the French people there is no more imperious duty'.

At the same time, however, the 18 June broadcast swiftly showed its ambivalent side, initially through its terminology. The resistance it alluded to (with a small r) was to become the Resistance (capital R), the day small groups of men and women in France itself, who rejected the armistice and Vichy, used the term as a sign of mutual recognition and as a statement. This is what happened, for example, on 15 December 1940 when a clandestine sheet was released in Paris, written and produced by the so-called *'Musée de l'Homme'* group, and bearing the title of *Résistance*. The term drew directly on the specific historical memory of the *Camisards*, since it was inspired by an inscription engraved in stone by Huguenot women who had been persecuted and imprisoned at Aigues-Mortes, in the tower of Constance: *'Résistez'*.

Furthermore, when de Gaulle had spoken of 'the flame of the French resistance', he was not thinking in terms of underground action, and even less of guerrilla warfare. What he had in mind was an engagement in classical military combat, in the external theatres of operations. After all, who at that time in France had heard of the inventors of guerrilla warfare, such as Michael Collins or Mao Tse-tung ? Who would have thought of drawing inspiration or lessons from their example? Indeed, de Gaulle himself, in his *Memoirs*, was the first to recognize this, with disarming frankness: 'The battlefield of underground action was, for all of us, entirely new'. And he went on, speaking from a primarily military outlook, based on intelligence and armed combat: 'In short, there was nothing in metropolitan France to which our action could attach itself. The service which was to operate on this special field of battle would have to be drawn out of the void'.[2] At the time, the only elements on French soil that were really prepared for underground action were the communists, by virtue of the training in revolutionary tactics given them by the Comintern, and of their experience during the inter-war period .

From the very outset, then, a division was evident between the external and the internal Resistance; and, common enemy notwithstanding, the conditions of the struggle, the mentalities that lay behind it and the operating methods used, were in each case dramatically different. The basic dilemma was, therefore, whether these two currents would flow their own separate ways without ever meeting, with all the risks of rivalry

[2]Charles de Gaulle, *War Memoirs; Vol. 1, The Call to Honour 1940–1942* (1954; English translation: Collins, London, 1955), p.155.

and dispersion of effort that this entailed, or whether they would at some stage come together. And if the latter were to occur, who would take command? In other words, from the very beginning, the seeds were sown for numerous potential conflicts between the two Resistances – external and internal, Free France and the French underground movement – so great were the differences and divergences between the two in terms of historical experiences, sensibilities and aims.

In fact, the division extended far beyond the immediate war years, for its heritage and memory have never ceased to be sources of antagonism between the French since 1945. The lines of division between the men in London and the men of the shadows, between the Gaullists of Free France and the resistance fighters of the interior, which were born in the struggle itself and reinforced by suffering, have survived down through the years, and the passing of time has done nothing to bridge the gap. To this day, these antagonisms can still be clearly perceived, and they resurface periodically as 'replays' of collective memory, which can on occasion go very deep. A striking example of this was seen in 1989, when the publication of Daniel Cordier's book on Jean Moulin rekindled old divisions and reopened wounds of forty years ago. The protagonists passionately divided into two camps, according to their positions at the time, some on the side of London, others on the side of the resistance movements in France.[3]

As for 1940 itself, let us first of all look beyond the imagery which collective memory has magnified and mythified out of all proportion, and remind ourselves just how humble the beginnings of both the London-based Gaullist movement and the internal Resistance were. Co-ordination between the two posed almost insurmountable problems in the early days, and communications were difficult to establish on either side of the Channel. As a result each side was necessarily cloistered off in its own world. In France, whether in the 'free' zone or the occupied zone, everything had to be improvised. The earliest structures of the Resistance were closer to what Jean-Pierre Azéma has so aptly described as 'a sort of do-it-yourself affair'. Very early on, admittedly, a wave of sympathy towards London could be noted, made up of a mixture of anglophilia and gaullophilia. The practice of tuning in to the BBC came to represent both a manifestation and a symbol of this sympathy. But at this early stage, if Gaullism (which some prefects still called 'De Gaullism') was symptomatic of a state of mind, it hardly described an organized movement. Small and scattered groups assembled here and there. 'Vive de Gaulle' could be seen written in chalk on a number of walls.

---

[3]D. Cordier, *Jean Moulin: l'inconnu du Panthéon.*; Vol. 1. *Une ambition pour la République: juin 1899–juin 1936*; Vol. 2 *Le choix d'un destin: juin 1936–novembre 1940* (Lattès, Paris, 1988 and 1989).

The first underground publications began to appear in the summer of 1940 – for example, Jean Texcier's *Conseils à l'occupé*. Yet as late as December the first typewritten issue of *Libération-Nord*, launched by trade unionists, had only seven copies run off! It is true that at the time the *Musée de l'Homme* group, composed mainly of intellectuals – scholars, writers and lawyers – began to take shape and to acquire an ideological and political dimension. Alongside the network of escape channels it organized, it also edited the paper *Résistance*. But by February–March 1941, the group was disbanded following betrayal, its leaders arrested and subsequently shot. Moreover, it could in no way be described as Gaullist. The same can be said of the southern zone, where neither Captain Frenay's *Mouvement de Libération Nationale* (later to become *Combat*), nor *Libération*, launched by left-wing elements, nor *Liberté*, run by Christian democrats, made any more than passing reference to de Gaulle. As for the communists, if one follows the official line, he was actually the target of their attacks, perceived as the servant of British capitalism and of 'the City', at least until the creation of the National Front in spring 1941. Then the invasion of the Soviet Union changed the whole situation.

In spite of everything, there were faint signs of movement in a country which was enslaved and still reeling from the shock of defeat. Alongside spontaneous initiatives from small groups seeking each other out, and helped by the general refusal to collaborate, some of the orders issued from London met with favourable reactions. The silent demonstration held on 1 January 1941 was more widely observed than Carlton Gardens had hoped. More importantly, on 11 November 1940, while two lawyers, Weil-Curiel and Nordmann, placed a spray of flowers at the foot of Clemenceau's statue, accompanied by a card reading: 'From General de Gaulle', an important protest demonstration took place on the Champs-Elysées, which brought together not only students, but men and women of all ages, and from all walks of life. All in all, though, 1940 was a year that saw the emergence of more sympathizers than activists.

Meanwhile, in London the initial activities of Free France seemed scarcely more encouraging, and achieved only modest results. One has only to think of the numbers of the Free French Army – barely 30,000 men by the end of 1940. De Gaulle, alluding to these difficult beginnings, spoke of 'the terrible weakness with which we were struggling'. He himself was certainly a stylish incarnation of a struggling country. He boldly proclaimed himself to be the leader, not of a foreign legion based in Great Britain, but of the French nation at war: 'We *are* France', he declared to René Cassin. The magical quality of the verb and the power of the myth will not, however, impress the historian. Ultimately, de Gaulle might well seek to set himself up as the symbol (as he was to be dubbed by Emmanuel d'Astier de la Vigerie) and the paradigm of the continuing struggle; but he was nonetheless fully aware of the general passivity prevailing amongst the majority of the French people. 'We were forced to recognise', he wrote, 'that, in both zones, opinion inclined to passivity ... no sign led one to suppose that French people in appreciable numbers were resolved on action ... . At bottom, the great majority wanted to believe that Pétain was playing a deep game and that, when the day came, he would take up arms again. The general opinion was that he and I were secretly in agreement. In the last resort, propaganda had, as always, only slight value in itself. Everything depended on events.'[4] One is reminded of the rather cruel assessment of 1940 made by that great *résistant*, Jean Cassou: 'Everybody packed up and went home'.

Furthermore, relations between London and France could only be established with the help of the English, and that caused problems, despite the best efforts of the *deuxième bureau* – or military intelligence – of Free France, which was later to form the original core of *BCRA* (*Bureau Central de Renseignement et d'Action*). Thus it was that the earliest message sent back by one of the first agents to land in France, Lieutenant-Commander d'Estienne d'Orves, is dated as late as December 1940. It was not until September 1941 that the first Lysander landed from England.

The situation improved somewhat in the course of 1941. Signs of resistance were developing in two directions, but without necessarily conflicting with support for Pétain, which remained strong. On the one hand, the intelligence networks set up by Free France were developed and expanded, in spite of obstacles and losses such as that of d'Estienne d'Orves and his assistants, who were shot in August 1941. In fact a full-scale intelligence war evolved, through the impetus given by Captain Dewavrin (alias Passy), who created a network of agents directing voluntary informers in France. The first group of these agents, sent from London, used the names of metro stations on the Etoile-Nation line as pseudonyms: Passy himself, Saint-Jacques, Corvisart and so on. However, in this intelligence war directed from England, the networks operated by the Free French found themselves in competition, and often in conflict with, the British networks of MI6 (Military Intelligence) and of the SOE (Secret Operations Executive), which made life rather difficult for them. The other form taken by the internal Resistance was that of improvised groups which emerged spontaneously in various places, and expanded as time went on. They were notably strengthened by communist participation from the summer of 1941 onwards, at a time when German repression was growing increasingly severe, with frequent arrests, reprisals and executions. However, most of these 'movements' (a label they themselves adopted) swore no allegiance to Gaullism, whether they were organizations operating in the occupied zone (such as *Organisation Civile et Militaire, Défense de la France, Résistance*, etc.) or

[4]De Gaulle, *Call to Honour*, pp.159–160.

the trinity of *Combat, Libération & Franc-Tireur* in the southern zone.

In short, between the summer of 1940 and the beginning of 1942, the internal Resistance and the external Resistance, the underground movements and Free France (excluding the various networks), tended to follow divergent paths rather than co-ordinate their activity. It is hardly surprising, then, that the first contacts between the internal Resistance and de Gaulle proved to be delicate, sometimes mistrustful, and very quickly open to conflict – all the more so because de Gaulle was convinced that the direction, the impetus and the unity necessary to the movement had to come from Free France. On this point – even if it was not often perceived at the time – we can find several declarations made by him in the course of 1941, all of them significant in their unambiguous and somewhat authoritarian insistence on the necessary submission of the resistance movement to the orders of the leader of Free France: 'The organisation and direction of this resistance', he declared, 'not only in the territories already freed, but throughout France and the Empire, is the foremost task that the French National Committee has set itself'.[5] On another occasion, he spelled things out even more clearly, demanding discipline and obedience from the resistance within France: 'The war of the French people must be led by their leaders – in other words, by myself and the National Committee. All those fighting, whether in France or abroad, must follow orders to the letter'.[6]

It is understandable, therefore, that relations between de Gaulle and the internal Resistance should have appeared disconcerting to the latter, and often have led to mutual misunderstandings and confusion. The gulf separating the two sides is rather well illustrated by the encounter between Jean Moulin, who returned from London on 2 January 1942 as de Gaulle's 'ambassador', endowed with full powers, and Henri Frenay, the leader of *Combat*, who was angered by what he called 'not opinions, or suggestions, but nothing less than instructions of an extremely precise nature, right down to the smallest detail. In fact, they are orders'.[7] From that point on, clashes were to arise continually, fuelled by what Francis Louis Closon has rightly called 'the almost complete ignorance of each wing of the Resistance with regard to the other'.[8]

[5]Speech given in London on 2 October 1941, at a dinner organized by the international press, in de Gaulle, *Discours et messages;* Vol. 1, *Pendant la guerre, juin 1940–janvier 1946* (Plon, Paris, 1970), p.112.
[6]Speech given on the BBC on 23 October 1941, cited in de Gaulle, *Discours et messages* , 1, p.123.
[7]H. Frenay, *The Night Will End* (1973; English translation: Abelard-Schuman, London, 1976) p.124.
[8]F. L. Closon, *Le temps des passions: de Jean Moulin à la Libération* (Presses de la Cité, Paris, 1974) p.64.

During 1942, however, things were to evolve gradually under the force of circumstances. Firstly because, notwithstanding all the obstacles, the support given de Gaulle by the Resistance was on the increase – and this support came more from the lower end of the movement than the upper, for the need for unity was making itself felt most powerfully among the rank-and-file. For his part, the leader of the Free French, fighting on several fronts, but in particular to establish his legitimacy with the allies, made consummately skilful use of the moral and political support given to him so freely by the Resistance within France. The fact was that this support had now become vital to de Gaulle's strategy towards the English and the Americans. Witness, for example, the words of Pierre Brossolette, explaining this necessity very plainly to André Philip and urging him to rally the support of the socialist rank-and-file for de Gaulle: 'What de Gaulle needs, indeed, is tangible and undeniable proof of the existence of Gaullism in France; ... what you must supply, publicly and visibly (and I shall tell you how, shortly) is a demonstration of the unreserved gaullism of the socialist masses'. And Brossolette adds that 'by the gesture he made in 1940, de Gaulle has become the moral leader, indeed the outright leader of France, and for that very reason he is the right person to oversee the task of getting the country back onto its feet'.[9]

The decisive turning-point here was the period from January to June 1943, the time of the confrontation with General Giraud, whom the Anglo-Americans were stubbornly trying to support against de Gaulle. De Gaulle's response was to set up, under the responsibility of Jean Moulin, the National Council of the Resistance (CNR). This was brought about with some difficulty, in the middle of a serious crisis for leaders of the various resistance movements, and it brought certain of them into violent opposition to Moulin. However, in so far as the work of Daniel Cordier has shed considerable light on this episode, there is no need for us to dwell on it at length here.[10] It is important, however, to underline three important lessons which emerged from this crucial period. Firstly, if the unification of the resistance movement appeared so necessary, it was not simply as a temporary and tactical operation, but rather as a step towards enabling the external Resistance – personified by de Gaulle, and backed up by the internal Resistance – to win back control of the country's destiny. To put it another way, if current events dictated the line to be followed, their future implications were even more important, for what was fundamentally at stake was the control of power in France

[9]Letter from Pierre Brossolette to André Philip, 30 May 1942, quoted in Colonel Passy, *Souvenirs; vol. 2,10 Duke Street Londres (Le BCRA)* (Raoul Solar, Monte-Carlo, 1947), pp.220 and 225.
[10]See *Jean Moulin et le Conseil National de la Résistance* (CNRS/Institut d'Histoire du Temps Présent, Paris, 1983); Cordier, *Jean Moulin*, Vol. 1.

after the Liberation. This was why, in his instructions addressed to Jean Moulin on 7 May 1943 ordering him immediately to set up the CNR, de Gaulle could write without hesitation: 'For you it will be a matter of taking power – against the Germans, against Vichy, against Giraud, and perhaps against the allies'.[11] Secondly, since the CNR had from its first session pledged unreserved allegiance to de Gaulle, he could from then onwards boast a double legitimacy – national and political – thanks to the alliance achieved, albeit at the cost of terrible struggles, between the resistance movements and the political parties, all of which were represented on the council. This constituted an irreversible process, the credit for which was due in the first instance to Jean Moulin, whose doggedly loyal and efficient services were the shaping force behind it. Thirdly, even if the majority of the Resistance had now rallied *en masse* behind de Gaulle, the split between the leaders of some of the movements in the southern zone was to leave lasting traces. So it was for Henri Frenay, who in his memoirs related the tense exchange he had at that time with de Gaulle, in a scene which has since become famous. To de Gaulle's announcement that 'I shall give orders', Frenay retorted: 'General, the action in which we are engaged in France has two aspects which are inseparable, yet very different in nature. On the one hand, in the secret army and the *groupes francs*, we are soldiers, and as such ... it goes without saying that we will obey. In other respects, we are citizens free to think and act as we wish. We cannot relinquish this freedom of judgement, which means that as far as your orders in this domain are concerned, we shall choose whether or not to obey'. De Gaulle remained silent for a few moments , and then replied 'Well then, Charvet [Frenay's pseudonym], France will choose between you and me'.[12]

The second decisive moment was to come with the spring and summer of 1944, on the eve, and in the wake, of the allied landing. From here onwards, everything was rather rushed under the pressure of events.

On the other side of the Resistance, the second half of 1943 had been costly and gloomy. Beginning with the arrest and subsequent death of Jean Moulin, it had continued with acts of repression from all quarters which had caused heavy losses both in the ranks of the movements and the networks. At the same time, a certain sense of discouragement was emerging in the minds of the people. The long awaited allied landing – 'before the leaves fall' Churchill had said – had not yet happened. Weariness was gaining ground. Nevertheless, the Resistance fighters could

[11]Closon, *Le temps des passions*, p.65.
[12]Frenay, *La nuit finira. Mémoires de la résistance 1940–1945* (Laffont, Paris, 1973) , pp.256–7. The translation of this given in Frenay, *The Night Will End,* differs slightly from the version given here.

draw some degree of consolation from the weakening of the Vichy regime. Indeed, at the beginning of 1944, try as it might to keep up appearances, Vichy's authority was crumbling on all sides, and it was increasingly losing control over the instruments of power, essentially the administration, the police and the *gendarmerie*.

At this stage, three main considerations governed the prospects of the Liberation, which everybody felt to be imminent, and introduced a new element into the relations between the Resistance and de Gaulle, bringing them closer together, in a way that led to the triumph of the summer of 1944. The first problem was political: which force was going to take power in France after the Liberation? Everybody was in agreement as to the principle, and the common call was: 'give power back to the French people'. But what did that mean in concrete terms? On the side of the allies, whose military power would carry out the Liberation, there was great confusion. Admittedly, from the very first agreements signed with the Free French on 7 August 1940, the British had undertaken to restore completely 'the independence and greatness of France'. In the American camp, however, many imagined de Gaulle to be a dangerous dictator set on imposing his rule on the French people. Others (in some cases, the same people) feared a chaotic and indiscriminate witch-hunt which could plunge France into a blood-bath. In March 1944, the execution of Pucheu in Algiers, vociferously called for by the Resistance movement, confirmed them in their view.

Most importantly of all, there was the problem of the communists. Was de Gaulle simply another Kerensky who was going to be manipulated by the communists, or would he manipulate them? Leading circles in the United States might well have finally abandoned the idea that he was nothing more than a British puppet, but they were still extremely wary of the 'red threat', convinced as they were that there was a strong risk of revolution in France, which they regarded as a country doomed to political unrest, the settling of scores, and anarchy. As far as this analysis was concerned, the British differed perceptibly from the Americans, since their reasoning was quite the reverse. From their point of view, Gaullism appeared as the only credible alternative to communism – an argument that de Gaulle himself would not fail to use, pointing out that if the allies did not support him they would be throwing not only the Resistance, but the whole of France, straight into the arms of the communists.

On this question, the same lines of division, the same questions and the same reasoning were to be found within the internal Resistance. For the leaders primarily, but also for many of the rank-and-file Resistance fighters, the main question was whether or not the liberation would be the signal for an attempt by the Communist Party to seize power, given the key role it had played in the Resistance since 1941 and the powerful position it still commanded within the movement. Today, thanks to the work of Annie Kriegel, Maurice Agulhon and Philippe Buton, we know that the communists' strategy was a complex one, with several layers and a variable schedule, which was not directed towards the straight-forward seizure of power that people feared at the time. The undeni-able result, however, was a *rapprochement* between de Gaulle and the non-communist (and sometimes *anti*-communist) majority in the Resistance.

Another debate was absolutely crucial in terms of the tactics to be pur-sued before and during the Liberation, added to the divisions within the internal Resistance and created further links with de Gaulle's strategy; this was the question of armed struggle. Here there were those in favour of immediate action – a sort of generalized agitation for armed action – which included the Communist Party and certain activist elements of the Resistance. Then there were those who deemed it pointless to risk incurring massacres in this way, and whose approach, especially in the case of the *maquis*, consisted of holding out until 'D-Day' before going into action – hence the accusations since made against them of having played a waiting game. Among the latter could be counted most of the leading figures of the non-communist resistance, as well as de Gaulle and the CFLN (*Comité Français de Libération Nationale*).

The third issue at stake was the question of the organization of the new powers in post-Liberation France, a debate in which there were serious disagreements between de Gaulle and the internal Resistance fighters. In theory, the edict of 10 January 1944 had settled this by creating *Commissaires de la République* as representatives and agents of the central authority at regional level, the *Comités Départementaux de Libération* along-side the prefects at departmental level, representing the various strands of the Resistance, and *Comités Locaux de Libération* at local level.

In the spring of 1944, in the heady atmosphere of the eve of combat, more fanciful ideas emerged. In the minds of many Resistance fighters, the Liberation had by now taken on all the proportions of a Second Com-ing. As far as they were concerned, the revolutionary dynamic gener-ated by their actions and sacrifices had to be followed through to the very end. Bright new tomorrows were imagined for a new France, puri-fied and transformed from top to bottom, united in fraternal harmony under the leadership of new men – many of whom had emerged from the ranks of the Resistance – and entirely devoted to the good of the people. It was a mood well captured by an American historian:[13] 'In a brilliant and prodigious press, written in the inimitable elegance of classical

---

[13]G. Kolko, *The Politics of War: Allied Diplomacy and the World Crisis of 1943–1945* (Ran-dom House, New York, 1968), p.79.

French style, articulate with ideas but relatively silent with guns before spring 1944, the Resistance possessed eloquence and pathos in its impotence, but it held out the promise, and threat, of action'.

General de Gaulle, for his part, as the unwavering defender of the nation since 1940, had assigned himself three priorities – sovereignty, the state, and greatness. Sovereignty entailed absolute respect for national independence, notwithstanding the prostration which had followed defeat. This was a sacred heritage which had to be vigilantly defended against any attempted encroachment from without. The state, the secular backbone of French unity, symbolized the authority of a governing central power which had to be restored as swiftly as possible. As for France's standing in the world, this came to be identified with the greatness which now had to be recovered, since, according to de Gaulle's orthodoxy, 'France cannot be France without greatness'.

However, it was precisely these three essential requirements – sovereignty, the state, and greatness – which had been repeatedly challenged and threatened by allied policy, which was always quick to take advantage of the weakened situation of France. This explains de Gaulle's implacable attitude, on his own admission condemned to refuse all compromise: 'The weaker I am', he explained to a Resistance fighter who had just arrived from France, 'the more intransigent I shall be in defending our rights and getting them respected'.[14] He had applied himself unflaggingly to this task with a brusqueness and tough-mindedness which had continually exasperated his partners and had led his opponents to describe him either as ungrateful or paranoid. Henceforth, this haughty and mistrustful solitude became for him a sort of rule of existence, which had affected his relations with the Resistance leaders who, when they arrived in London or in Algiers, were stunned to learn of his disputes with the British and Americans.

On the allied side, it must be said, there had been no shortage of snubs and other displays of bad manners, sometimes going as far as the most brutal manœuvres, aimed at getting rid of a character who was seen as both an obstacle and a nuisance. Things had started to turn sour with the British as early as 1941, but it was with the Americans that the lack of understanding had been most keenly felt, and where the support of the Resistance movement for him became an indispensable and decisive trump card. As far as Roosevelt was concerned, the picture was indeed a very clear one: since its defeat, France was finished as a country and could be struck off the list of world powers for at least another twenty-five years. As for de Gaulle, he found him exasperating, with his airs of grandeur and his patently ridiculous and anachronistic pretensions. As

---

[14]Interview with Félix Gouin given in Gibraltar, cited in J. R. Tournoux, *Pétain and de Gaulle* (1964; English translation: Heinemann, London, 1966), p.158.

for the future of the French after the landing and the Liberation, he personally envisaged nothing more than the status of a military administration: 'I am inclined to think', he had written to Churchill in spring 1943, 'that when we get into France itself we will have to regard it as a military occupation run by British and American generals ... . This may be necessary for six months or even a year'.[15] The most telling indication of the depth and persistence of this prejudice against de Gaulle is to be found, a full twenty years later, in the words of Charles Bohlen, who was none the less one of the most brilliant minds at work in Roosevelt's team. Having been appointed American ambassador in Paris in 1963, he continued, in a report to Washington, to describe Charles de Gaulle as the perfect representative of all that was conservative, hierarchical, religious and militarist in France.[16]

Because of this, only one line of conduct was possible for de Gaulle: that of order and unity under the CFLN and its leader, symbol of sovereignty, of the state and of its national standing. There might well be unanimity between the Resistance fighters and Algiers on the principle of French sovereignty in the liberated territories, and on the right of the French to participate in the liberation of their country, as allies in their own right and as citizens of a free and independent state. But when it came to the restoration of national greatness, with the French bluntly denying the allied military command any powers of political decision-making or territorial administration, a great many sticking-points still remained between an imperious and intransigent de Gaulle and the impatient activists of the Resistance, sure in their own minds of the rights they had paid for so dearly in blood and tears. This was the reason why, in Algiers, he was careful to continually remind his 'soldiers without uniform' of their duty to obey, and his own representatives of their responsibility as servants of the state. This attitude is nowhere better expressed than in the directives that he gave in July 1944 to his delegate-general in France, Alexandre Parodi: 'You are the representative of the government. This means that your instructions must, in the last instance, be listened to ... . I recommend that you always speak very loudly, and very clearly, in the name of the state. The many forms and various actions of our admirable internal Resistance are means by which our nation has fought for its salvation. The state comes above all of these forms and all of these actions'.[17]

In these conditions, when the liberation came, between June and September 1944, the die was already cast. The power merger which had

[15]W. F. Kimball, ed., *Churchill and Roosevelt: The Complete Correspondence*, 2, (Princeton University Press, 1984), p.210, letter of 8 May 1943.
[16]C. Bohlen, *Witness to History* (Norton, New York, 1973), p.502.
[17]See J. Soustelle, *Envers et contre tout*; Vol.2, *D'Alger à Paris. Souvenirs et documents sur la France Libre 1942–1944* (Robert Laffont, Paris, 1950), p.421.

been months in preparation was accomplished without too many differences of opinion between the Resistance forces and the head of the provisional government. It must be admitted that the *Zeitgeist* was favourable to union, to such an extent that one can genuinely speak of a honeymoon between de Gaulle and the Resistance movement – a fleeting one, but one that was none the less real and widespread.

Now the time had come to harvest the fruits of the effort made on all sides, when the organization of powers in post-Liberation France had been established by agreement between Algiers and the internal Resistance, but without any consultation with the allies. This established *Commissaires de la République*, prefects and committees of liberation, all of whom were appointed at the appropriate time. So that in every region liberated by the allied forces, new authorities took power without encountering any difficulties, secure in the knowledge that they enjoyed overwhelming public support.

There were two phases to this process – firstly in Normandy and the West, and then in the Midi. The 'Norman model' served as a sort of trial attempt. Here there was a general rallying of the population to de Gaulle, behind the provisional government envoys on the one hand (François Coulet as *Commissaire de la République* and Pierre de Chevigné as *délégué militaire*), and the local Resistance leaders on the other. In the second phase, in August, it was the turn of the Midi – and the red Midi turned out to be an obedient Midi. For here too, the new authorities took up their positions in an atmosphere of national cohesion and efficiency earning them the praise of the American officers of civilian affairs, who sent their superiors very reassuring reports on the situation. There was only one exception – Monaco, where the Prince and the Prime Minister, exasperated by the FFI and the FTP, called together the American generals in the sector to propose placing the principality under American protection – an offer which was politely declined! In short, 'republican legality' was restored throughout the territory.

The high point was the liberation of Paris. For de Gaulle, the parade on 26 August 1944, in which the people, the Resistance fighters and the head of the provisional government marched together in shared emotional fervour, represented a genuine coronation, democratic and mystic in its character, creating links with the royal and religious coronation previously held in Reims. From that point on the allies, who until then had obstinately refused to recognize the provisional government, formally did so, thereby consecrating a victory for de Gaulle and acknowledging the unanimous support that he had from the entire Resistance movement. At the end of the day, unity and discipline had prevailed among the ranks of the Resistance fighters, in spite of their internal divisions and disagreements. Behind a façade of flamboyant rhetoric, the individual leaders had managed to show political maturity; and in the course of this crucial period, the mystique of the Resistance had managed to evolve into a reasoned and well-constructed political agenda.

This union of minds, however, did not last. Within the space of four weeks, de Gaulle and the Resistance parted ways again. In de Gaulle's view, the time had come to assert central authority again – with watchwords such as the restoration of the state, the restoration of order and the restoration of national status in face of the continued threat from the allies. Such priorities, however, left most members of the Resistance with the feeling they had been swindled. Now that there was no further need for their alliance, which had been a temporary and tactical one formed specifically for the Liberation, de Gaulle appeared to them to be a monster of ingratitude. Emmanuel d'Astier de la Vigerie, the head of the *Libération* movement, and de Gaulle's Minister of the Interior in Algiers, related the terms in which de Gaulle had explained to him that he would be replaced once they were back in Paris: 'We've had enough of this fanciful resistance of yours; the government is here now ... and what we need is order!'[18]

Moreover, de Gaulle continued to act in the same proud and inflexible manner, alienating members of the Resistance still further. From his point of view , there was no reason whatever for the state to show gratitude towards them, since they had a natural duty to serve it. Already in London, Pierre Brossolette, whose Resistance credentials were impeccable, had criticized de Gaulle's way of treating people, pointing out that his harsh and insensitive attitude tended to discourage even his most devoted followers.[19] Julian Jackson has also emphasized the sense of disappointment, and sometimes even of hurt, that many Resistance heroes who had made great personal sacrifices experienced at their first meeting with him. Indeed some of them had not hidden their feelings. Shortly before leaving for France on the mission from which he was never to return, Jacques Bingen, for example, had warned him 'All men are not equally worthy of contempt'.[20]

None the less, beyond these difficulties related to character and personal sensitivities, at the very centre of the antagonisms which were to separate de Gaulle and the Resistance movement, there lay two basic difficulties. The first was political. In direct contradiction to the Resistance, which sought to prolong its existence by continuing as an active force within the newly-formed Fourth Republic, de Gaulle intended to pursue a strategy designed to restore order and respect for the authority of

---

[18]E. d'Astier de la Vigerie, *Seven Times Seven Days* (1947; English translation: MacGibbon & Kee, London, 1958), p.183.
[19]See A. Chambon, *Quand la France était occupée* (Editions France-Empire, Paris, 1987), pp.100–3.
[20]See J. Jackson, *Charles de Gaulle* (Cardinal, London, 1990), p.110.

the state, personified by himself. Restoration in the face of revolution? The debate cannot be expressed in such simplistic terms. However, it is undeniable that there was a conflict between two different visions of the nation's future and, correspondingly, two different political strategies.

However, the conflict goes further than the clash of two sources of political legitimacy. It was also a conflict over representation and myth. In order to come into being, to establish its organizational structures and to ultimately triumph, Gaullism had needed to create its identity in terms of a myth, reinforced by the words of de Gaulle himself. The same process was also essential to the Resistance. Because of this, the lively and deep-rooted duality between the internal and external Resistance was evident from the outset, in 1940. From that moment on the struggle between the Gaullist myth and the Resistance myth, set in motion by the Liberation and kept alive by collective memory, has never ceased. It still endures today.

3

De Gaulle in Waiting
1946–1958

Jean-Pierre Rioux

There is no doubt that the period from 1946 to 1958 is neatly framed at either end by important political events. On 20 January 1946, General de Gaulle declared that he was 'leaving his post irrevocably'; ten months later, on 13 October, a Fourth Republic was born against his will, and with the rather meagre support of just one-third of the electorate. On 1 June 1958, the National Assembly appointed him as the last president of the council of the very regime he had always condemned. He was invested with full powers to draft a new constitution, which was subsequently adopted enthusiastically on 28 September with the support of 80 per cent of the votes cast.

In between these dates, the republic that de Gaulle detested had established itself, struggled against the odds, and then been slowly destroyed from the inside by the cancer of Algeria. France had been the only major nation to have had to bear the full brunt of the combined ravages of two upheavals on the world scene at home and abroad: the Cold War and decolonization.[1] But by 1958, reconstruction from the ruins of the Second World War had been completed, and economic growth and improved social conditions were already evident, due to the sheer hard work of the French population. Indeed, the 'dear old country' had probably done better than was believed or claimed by the voice emanating from Colombey. So, during these years, what were de Gaulle's expectations, and what did he do? This is the question that we must try to

---

[1]Jean-Pierre Rioux, 'Prologue', in F. Bloch-Lainé and J. Bouvier, eds., *La France restaurée (1944–1954)* (Fayard, Paris, 1986), pp.15–31.

answer, while striving to avoid stereotypes and taking into account the many gaps in the evidence.

Stereotypes? The most significant one is the inevitable designation of these years as the 'crossing of the desert', an expression which was quickly coined by some of the general's followers, and which passed into general usage. This was a 'crossing' which had to face up to alternating extremes of torrid heat and glacial cold but which, for de Gaulle's supporters, inevitably had to end up in the oasis of a new Gaullist republic. We should reject this view of inevitability, with its deliberate distortion of the record, and use the less pejorative phrase of a period of 'waiting' for these twelve years of history. 'In waiting' is the title aptly given to the edition of de Gaulle's *Discours et messages* [2] covering the period which concerns us here. First there was a period of disappointment, from 1946 to 1953; then a time of 'latency', the real 'crossing of the desert' from 1953 to 1958, following the failure of the Rassemblement du Peuple Français (RPF), about which there is rather less to be said.

As for the gaps in the evidence, they should not be overstated, since rapid progress has been made in the general history of these years.[3] However, the same cannot quite be said for the history of de Gaulle and Gaullism over the same period, for it has been somewhat overshadowed by the sheer bulk of publications dealing with the period of Free France and the Resistance on the one hand, and the subsequent years of the Fifth Republic on the other. This is despite the fact that the public and private archives are now open to examination, the essential memoirs of the period have been published, many of the protagonists of the time are still alive and prepared to give their recollections, and the best of de Gaulle's own autobiographical volumes is readily accessible. Despite the fact too that, as early as 1965, Christian Purtschet produced a good study of the organization of the RPF, that Jean Touchard has since analysed the ma-

[2]Charles de Gaulle, *Discours et messages*; Vol. 2, *Dans L'attente (février 1946–avril 1958)* (Plon, Paris, 1970). For all de Gaulle's own texts, see firstly *Memoirs of Hope. Renewal, 1958–1962* (1954; English translation: Weidenfeld & Nicolson, London, 1971); subsequently *Lettres, Notes et Carnets*; Vol. 6, *8 mai 1945–18 juin 1951* (Paris, Plon, 1984) and *Lettres, notes et carnets*; Vol. 7, *juin 1951–mai 1958* (Plon, Paris, 1985). Essential bibliographical material includes the following: Institut Charles de Gaulle, *Chronologie de la vie du général de Gaulle* (Plon, Paris, 1973); Institut Charles de Gaulle, *Bibliographie internationale sur Charles de Gaulle établie par l'Institut Charles de Gaulle (1940–1981)* (Institut Charles de Gaulle, Paris, 1981); Institut Charles de Gaulle, *Nouvelle bibliographie internationale sur Charles de Gaulle établie par l'Institut Charles-de-Gaulle* (Plon, Paris, 1990); J. Lacouture, *De Gaulle, 2, Le politique, 1945–1959* (Le Seuil, Paris, 1985). This volume of Lacouture's three-volume biography of de Gaulle has been translated in abridged form and merged with volume 3, as *De Gaulle, The Ruler 1945–1970* (Collins-Harvill, London, 1991)
[3]J.-P.Rioux, *The Fourth Republic, 1944–1958*. (1980–1983: English translation: Cambridge University Press, 1987)

jor texts of the period, that dissertations and theses have been written on the regional impact of Gaullism, and that Jean Charlot has published a preliminary synthesis of the period in his *Le gaullisme d'opposition*.[4]

The fact remains, however, that the period from 1946 to 1958 appears as something of a black hole, or at least a grey area, in the supposedly uninterrupted progress of the de Gaulle saga. The Gaullism of this bitter period of the Cold War years fits rather awkwardly into the story of the long and moving love affair between de Gaulle, France and the French. He himself, in his *Memoirs of Hope*, devotes only thirty-four rather dry lines to the six busy years prior to 1958, enabling him to depict himself – not without considerable exaggeration – as a solitary schemer, keeping watch over events during the final days before 13 May: 'At the time, I had completely retired from the scene, and was living at *La Boisserie*, where my door was open only to my family and a few people from the village. I only went to Paris occasionally, and there I was prepared to receive visitors only very infrequently'.[5]

So, although not completely ignored, this period in de Gaulle's life has been all too rarely studied, as if it represented some kind of blemish, a parenthesis, or a digression, in his career. Proof of this can be seen in the fact that even though de Gaulle today enjoys an exceptional and un-contested position in French collective memory, polls that have traced this development over the last twenty years show that it is because of his image as the man of 18 June 1940 and the sage of the Fifth Republic. It owes practically nothing to his role as the founder of the RPF, the hero whose legitimacy was then still latent.[6] Further proof, of a more limited but none the less significant nature, lies in the fact that among the enormous range of scholarly material brought together for the colloquium on *De Gaulle en son siècle*, held in Paris in November 1990, only one paper out of more than 150 presented addressed the period between 1946 and 1958, and that was the work of a Soviet historian.[7]

---

[4]In chronological order: C. Purtschet, *Le Rassemblement du peuple français 1947–1953* (Cujas, Paris, 1965); J. Touchard, *Le gaullisme 1940–1969* (Le Seuil, Paris, 1969); R. Rémond, *The Right Wing in France, from 1815 to de Gaulle*. (1968; English translation: University of Pennsylvania Press, Philadelphia, 1969); J. Charlot, *Le gaullisme d'opposition 1946–1958: histoire politique du gaullisme* (Fayard, Paris, 1983); P. Guiol, *L'impasse sociale du gaullisme. Le RPF et l'Action ouvrière* (Presses de la FNSP, Paris, 1985).

[5]De Gaulle, *Memoirs of Hope*, pp.15–16.

[6]See J.-P.Rioux, 'Le souverain en mémoire, 1969–1990', paper given at the colloquium on 'De Gaulle et son siècle' (Institut Charles-de Gaulle, Paris, forthcoming) and the analysis of the *SOFRES* opinion poll made by Raymond Barre, in O. Duhamel and J. Jaffré, eds., *L'état de l'opinion 1991* (Le Seuil, Paris, 1991).

[7]M. Arzakanian, 'Les gaullistes et la traversée du desert', lecture given at the colloquium on 'De Gaulle et son siècle' (Institut Charles-de Gaulle, Paris, November 1990).

'I am rebuilding Free France'

Yet these years form a link in a continuity extending back to the source – for it was then that a 'Gaullian' de Gaulle intimately embraced the 'Gaullism' inherent in the destiny of the RPF. However, the question immediately arises: can there be such a thing as a Gaullism of opposition, a sort of 'gaullism in waiting', with its leader demobilized while France entrusted its destiny to the followers of other philosophies of history? De Gaulle's answer to this question was in the affirmative, but had he fully perceived the difficulties and the promises of the new era ushered in by his withdrawal from affairs in 1946?[8] Another question has to be answered too. Had he the knowledge or the ability to handle the ambiguities of a period during which the Gaullist version of history had vanished, and when events were no longer under his control?

The third volume of his war memoirs, practically finished by 13 May 1958 and published in 1959, bears the trace of these initial questions. De Gaulle made no mention in them of the profound divisions his departure had caused in public opinion, and which were reflected in statistics from the Institut Français de l'Opinion Publique (41 per cent of the French in early 1946 believed that he had succeeded in his task, as against 36 per cent who said he had failed; 40 per cent were unhappy about his departure, as against 32 per cent satisfied and 28 per cent indifferent; 21 per cent thought that he would return to power, as against 43 per cent who said he was gone for good). He would later sum this up with a superb line: 'My popularity was like capital with which I could pay off the disappointments that were inevitable among the ruins'.[9]

However, although he was mistakenly convinced that popular pressure would soon bring him back to office, he also let it be understood, like a true army man, that it was very difficult to put a strategy of reconquest into practice when he had no control over the terrain or the timing. So, it was therefore better to use a tactic that went with the tide, while remaining alert for opportunities as they arose:

> Every Frenchman, whatever his tendencies, had the troubling suspicion that with the General had vanished something primordial, permanent and necessary which he incarnated in history, and which the regime of parties could not represent ... . They supposed such legitimacy could remain latent in a period without

---

[8]See J.-P.Rioux, 'De Gaulle en République, de Courseulles à Bayeux (1944–1946)', in P. Isoart and C. Bidegaray, eds., *Des Républiques françaises* (Economica, Paris, 1988), pp.695–703.
[9]Charles de Gaulle, *War Memoirs. Salvation, 1944–1946* (1959; English translation: London, Weidenfeld & Nicolson, 1960), p.14.

anxiety. But they knew it could be invoked by common consent as soon as a new laceration threatened the nation.[10]

Nevertheless, he was keen to reinforce this 'latent legitimacy' by constant reference back to the events of the war years, so keeping them alive in the public mind. The years between 1946 and 1958 therefore echoed to the noise of war memories, commemorations of Free France and the Resistance, the reactions of Resistance activists to the return to public life of Vichy supporters, or to the planned European Defence Community, regular visits to the martyrs of Mont-Valérien every 18 June, manifestos delivered from various symbolic landmarks or towns that had suffered during the victory over the enemy, efforts to keep the spirit of war comradeship alive and, as noted above, de Gaulle's creation of his own monument – his war memoirs.[11] During this period he certainly had a strategy with regard to collective memory which at times intersected with the history of the RPF, but never fully coincided with it. For it was by constantly harking back to the historic events of 1940 and to the triumphant events of August 1944 that de Gaulle intended to preserve his own stature as a leader and convince France of the need to return to the path of her great historical and moral destiny.

It was for this reason that during a visit from one of his close war companions early in 1947, he declared: 'I am rebuilding Free France – come with me!'. It was also the reason why, in the speech made at Bayeux on 16 June 1946 which heralded the new direction of a Gaullism in opposition, and which has remained famous for the constitutional propositions it contained, the past tense was so often used in describing the political agenda, the tactics and the plan for the battle ahead. It also used the terms of a war epic to describe the concern which was later to undermine the RPF: how were they to obtain the consent of the vast majority of the French to the absolute rule of an élite which had 'risen from nothing' by force and cunning, when the country was in the hands of another kind of republican political culture, that of the party system. Here is an extract from the Bayeux speech, which reveals a rather worrying sense of the ability of sheer will-power to govern events:

> Salvation came first of all from an élite which sprang up spontaneously from the depths of the nation and which, completely free of any preoccupations of party or class, devoted itself to the fight

[10]De Gaulle, *Salvation*, p.281.
[11]See H. Rousso, *The Vichy Syndrome: History & Memory in France since 1944* (1987; English translation: Harvard University Press, Cambridge Massachusetts, 1991); J.-P.Rioux, 'L'opinion publique française et la CED; querelle partisane ou bataille de la mémoire?', *Relations internationales*, February 1984, pp.37–53.

for the liberation of France and the restoration of her greatness. The psychology of this élite, which had risen from nothing and which despite heavy losses was to drag all of France and the Empire along in its wake, was characterized by a sense of its moral superiority, the awareness that it was fulfilling a sort of vocation of sacrifice and example, a passion for risk-taking and initiative, and a scornful contempt for agitation, pretensions and sensationalism. It also had supreme confidence, not only in the strength and the skill of its powerful organization, but also in its chances of victory and the future of the country. It would certainly not have succeeded, however, without the consent of the vast majority of the French people. [12]

The refrain was to be taken up again several times in the course of the party's life. For example, on 28 January 1950 in Marault (Haute-Marne), de Gaulle again claimed: 'Our party was created to engage the whole nation in this effort ... . In fact, it is something similar to what we did in the Resistance, when all over the country, in the midst of general apathy, we gradually built up a hard core of determined activists which finally succeeded bringing the whole nation along with it'.[13]

This deliberate anchoring of the movement in such a glorious view of the past was de Gaulle's work, for he knew full well how central it was to his own role, reflecting his integrity, along with his sense of historic mission and destiny which had to be protected at all costs. However, this loyalty and sense of mission had to be put into effect through the RPF, which he hoped to use to exact his political revenge and regain power. This brought him into the area of political tactics, and it would be an interesting historical exercise to trace in detail the origins and the first steps of this transition from the man of destiny to the man of partisan and electoral politics.

The launch of the RPF in Bruneval on 30 March, in Strasbourg on 7 April, in a *communiqué* of 14 April and a press conference ten days later, was not unlike an armoured attack. It came right in the middle of the Easter recess for the Chamber of Deputies, during the Joanovici and Hardy affairs[14], and before the real outbreak of the Cold War. It also followed months of meticulous preparation during the winter of 1946–7, when there had already been a confrontation between Malraux, who supported the creation of a movement based on spontaneous nationalism,

[12] De Gaulle, *Discours et messages, Dans l'attente*, p.6.
[13] De Gaulle, *Lettres, Notes, et Carnets, 1945–1961*, p.398.
[14] Joanovici was a metals merchant who had financed a Resistance organization while making a fortune from supplying the Germans. Hardy was a former Resister who was accused of complicity in betraying Jean Moulin to the Gestapo. Both cases therefore compromised the memory of the Resistance.

and Soustelle, who favoured a more cautious political approach. Meanwhile Rémy and Baumel had reinvigorated the members of the old Free French networks. Nevertheless this sensational launch of the movement came immediately after two strangely silent periods for de Gaulle which might also be interpreted as periods of tactical wavering and hesitation. The first of these was from January to June of 1946, from Marly to Bayeux, when he still thought that the loyalty of the *Mouvement républicain populaire* (MRP), however uncertain, might be sufficient to serve his needs. The second was from November 1946 to March 1947, a period marked only by his contemptuous announcement of 28 December 1946 that he would not be a contender for the presidency of the Fourth Republic.

It was true that in the meantime the MRP had betrayed him, three-party government had collapsed, a Third Force had taken shape and, most importantly, de Gaulle had failed to persuade the French to vote massively against the second constitutional referendum on 13 October 1946. All of this was probably enough to make it an opportune moment for the launch of the RPF, but day-to-day events had also played a part. After all, neither the sacking of communist ministers on 5 May 1947 nor the subsequent aggravation of the Cold War had been planned. Yet both had happened, in a country where nearly one in four of the electorate voted communist, and it was precisely this dramatic conjuncture that inspired a large part of the RPF's ambitions and its strength.

The principles 'which can save everything'

There is no need to explain in detail the complex, and often overlapping, organizational structures of the early RPF, or its major manœuvres during a period of dramatic growth, which brought it almost 38 per cent of the votes in the municipal elections of October 1947 – a peak from which it then rapidly declined. However, there can be no doubt that it succeeded in presenting a rational and vigorously argued overall plan for France which was coherent, and which contained all the main Gaullist ideas. In analysing this, an initial factor to bear in mind is the sense of impending disaster which persisted throughout the life of the RPF, and which would leave a visible trace, both in the Gaullism of 1958 and in that of the Fifth Republic. The RPF and its leader found themselves living at a time of new national uncertainty, like sailors navigating in a storm. They quickly mended the leaks in their own foundering ship, at a time when a new kind of war was just beginning – one which brought the Soviets within two stages of the Tour de France from France's eastern frontier, and which rapidly led to the defeat of the French expeditionary corps in Indochina, the division of Europe, and the emergence of bitter political conflict on the domestic scene. For de Gaulle and his followers the impact of the Cold War on France was aggravated by the fact that the country was on the brink of economic and financial collapse, bereft of captain or compass.

The RPF was not alone in gloomily prophesying an imminent crisis, but its leaders had grasped the extent to which this aura of impending doom dramatically reinforced the original driving force of war-time Gaullism. The original followers, who had never really been comfortable with the return of an old-style political life, now seemed to recover their old fire and welcomed with open arms anyone now willing to cling to the lifebelt that they offered. Yet playing on people's fear was not enough. The strength of the RPF also lay in its ability to offer a plan for salvation which matched the threat that the country faced. The definitive formulation of this plan only appeared in 1950, but its main points had been reiterated time and time again from the very beginning of the movement. The essential point had been made in the Strasbourg speech of 7 April 1947: 'The time has come to form and organize the *Rassemblement du Peuple Français* which, within the framework of the law, will rise above differences of opinion to promote and secure victory for a great effort of national salvation and the fundamental reform of the state'.[15] Legality and salvation, coupled with a rallying of people around a 'certain idea of France', were de Gaulle's remedy to the danger of national decline, or what he termed 'vegetating in the shadows'.

Added to this, naturally enough, was the fundamental factor referred to above, namely professed loyalty to the Resistance, reinforced with its ideal of national unity and its belief in a better future. The RPF represented 'fighting France' whose ambition, as Malraux would later say, was to 'give France back its soul'. This also meant that the battle would be about principles rather than ideology, since its aim was to incarnate the best of a France finally freed of party political divisions. These principles which, in de Gaulle's words, 'can save everything' proved difficult to define, but they were nevertheless crucially important and were best summarized by him at the first meeting of the National Council of the RPF in Paris on 19 July 1948:

> Faced with a situation of economic and social imbalance which has resulted in sharper class divisions than ever before, and a serious deficit in the combined productivity of French industry, we have a solution which is called Association. In response to the disintegration of the Empire which has already begun, we have a solution to offer which is called French Union. To the grave dan-

[15]De Gaulle, *Discours et messages, Dans l'attente*, p.55.

gers looming over Europe, the rest of the world, and ourselves, which are due to nothing other than Soviet Russia's ambitions for world domination, we have a solution called the European Federation, in both the economic and the defence areas. Finally, in response to the state of national collapse, we have a solution to offer which is the reform of the state.

Association, French Union, European Federation, and the reform of the state – these are all principles we espoused years ago, and I call you all as witnesses to the fact that we did so even at the worst moments of the recent war, when it seemed as though few people except ourselves were even concerned with the issues. And we did not just leave them at the level of principles: we defined them clearly too. Now, we have to translate these definitions into practical measures which can be implemented overnight, for that is probably what we will soon have to do.[16]

However vague these words may have been, and however imbued with de Gaulle's hypnotic voluntarism, their essential feature cannot be ignored: the quasi-military formulation of the four battle themes, with which the RPF believed it was heading for a final victory which would consecrate once and for all the ideal of mutual 'association between men, rather than conflict between their interests'. What is perhaps most interesting here is the expression of a kind of social moralism inherent in one of the four themes, which de Gaulle would return to again and again, that of the association of work and capital. This was much more than a sop to left-wing Gaullists who wore their heart on their sleeves, it was the very source of the popular – or populist – vigour of Gaullism. It also meant that de Gaulle accepted that the world of work and production was changing in the early years of the three decades of economic growth that followed the Second World War. It shows too his acceptance of the fact that world trade was in need of reorganization, and that the class struggle needed new rules and new solutions. In this respect, there was a genuinely modern outlook to his ideas which, it must be emphasized, preceded his bitter conflict with 'the scourge of separatism' and the Moscow dominated French Communist Party: a conflict which was to assume exceptional proportions within the RPF and become almost an obsession amongst its more militant members. The anti-communist stance of de Gaulle was therefore something fundamental, but it could not be separated from a positive social vision which, rightly or wrongly, he believed to be of paramount importance.

[16]De Gaulle, *Lettres, notes et carnets, 1945–1961*, p.281.

It was no coincidence, then, that in one of his later speeches which sums up the movement's philosophy rather well, he placed it at the top of the list of his 'three flames of France' which were the burning inspiration of the RPF . Here is the best-known passage from the speech, which he delivered in Saint-Maurice on the 11 February 1950:

> There are three flames in France, all three of which have in one way or another made the French nation what it is, and which we must have with us and amongst us.
>
> There is first of all what I will call the social flame; the flame of those who reject social injustice and wish to ensure that every French citizen has his place and his share in France, and that all men have their dignity. This is our flame.
>
> Then there is the specifically Christian flame, which comes essentially from the same source as the first. Specifically Christian, for the fact is that we are a Christian country, and have been for a very long time. As a result, we have been more or less – but rather more than less – shaped by this flame. There is no reason not to see ourselves for what we are, and so, in its human and moral dimensions, this too is our flame.
>
> Finally, there is the flame of tradition. This is something which exists, and indeed must exist, in our country. We cannot build France by constantly denying our past; everything hangs together. We come from a source in the past and as Jaurès used to say – I am not afraid to quote him – we are headed towards the sea. We are a river flowing towards the sea, but in doing so we intend to be true to our source. The flame of tradition is also indispensable in order to rebuild a great country, and this too is our flame.
>
> These are the three real sources of inspiration which we wish to keep with us and which must emphatically be used together if we are to rebuild our country in the terrible circumstances of the present day.[17]

'The collapse of illusions'

However, these noble long-term ambitions were translated into rather mediocre tactics, and this was precisely the tragedy of the RPF. For the force of events and the pressure of opposition were such that its original ideas had to be hastily watered down in an attempt to stay on course. Some of them, admittedly, stood up well to the pressure, especially the

---

[17]De Gaulle, *Lettres, notes et carnets, 1945–1961*, pp.405–6.

drive against communism. The struggle against 'this cancer close to the heart of France', which was so evident in clashes at public meetings or on municipal councils where RPF members sat alongside members of the Communist Party (PCF) and of the *Confédération générale du travail* (CGT), was always dependent on an international situation where the menace of Stalinist Russia loomed large on the world scene. The same firmness was apparent in relation to other key themes of domestic politics, for example in the hostility shown towards the political parties of 'croaking frogs', and towards the regime which 'bobbed about above the country like a cork on the surface of the sea'. The same unswerving loyalty to the institutional solutions proposed in the Bayeux speech remained in evidence, and the internal constitution of the RPF was meant to be a sort of first application of these solutions.

On the other hand, it is not difficult to identify a series of perceptible changes in de Gaulle's attitude toward the United States. Openly favourable to the Atlantic alliance in 1947, he subsequently expressed increasingly strong reservations which became decidedly bitter during the European Defence Confederation controversy. As regards European policy, even if his support for a European confederation which 'could be the West's last chance' remained firm, the application of this idea to the German problem saw his position change from support for the dismantling of Germany and for measures to prevent its future rearmament, to the welcoming of Adenauer as the 'good German'. More spectacular still were the changes towards the French Union, over the 1947 statute for Algeria and over government policy in Indochina. Here, the war effort was still being supported in 1953, but the strategy of withdrawal that was adopted in Geneva in the following year by Pierre Mendès-France was never repudiated.

In fact, policy variations were not what was responsible for the final collapse of the RPF. After all, all the other political groups had also been put off balance by the new and dangerous world that had emerged in the post-war world. We should therefore probably look rather at the individuals concerned, and at their involvement in the political struggle, if we wish to uncover the deeper causes of the powerlessness of the RPF. For most of its internal history was epitomized by its growing inability to resolve the structural contradictions inherent in its origins. How could one bring people together while simultaneously operating a policy of exclusion and rejection? How could one participate effectively in political debate while refusing to be a political party like the others? How could the initial ruling of 13 November 1947 which made all elected office within the RPF incompatible with office at national or local level be imposed? Was it any surprise that local elected representatives should have succumbed to the delights of playing the party game, when many of them had not been prepared to resolve the delicate problem of double allegiance by resigning from office? Or that the RPF members of the Chamber of Deputies should have given themselves complete freedom to discuss issues and table proposals? De Gaulle, who for some time had been reticent and short of arguments, finally yielded to their pressures in June 1949. In this way, battle-weary parliamentarians were at last able to enter the executive and administrative commissions of the RPF, to the great fury of Malraux. A similar analysis could be made of the regrettable tactical handling of another initial contradiction, whereby the RPF, although not prepared to be a party like the others, still competed against them at every election, while refusing to risk any illegal action. At both the municipal elections of 1947, which brought dazzling results, and the disappointing legislative elections of 1951, this profound contradiction was not confronted, and the consequences of this oversight were that several of those elected 'took soup' and behaved like the other Fourth Republic politicians.

Admittedly, it can be argued in defence of the RPF and de Gaulle that operating as they did within a very legalistic republican framework, they had no control over the electoral calendar or over the various ways of manipulating the voting results through changes in the voting system. It is true that the Third Force was entitled to delay the date of the election or to create groupings of electoral lists which worked to their own advantage. It is also true that the RPF was violently taken to task, notably by the communists, and that in reaction to this the social profile of Gaullists began to lean to the right, even without considering the questionable rallying to its cause of former Vichy supporters. But in the case of the controversy over the electoral system, or the revival of the controversy over Catholic schools in 1950 and 1951 (which certainly weakened the Third Force but also considerably hastened the rallying of Gaullist representatives to the potential new centre-right majority) one cannot help wondering whether better tactical precautions might not have been taken. So much so, perhaps, that even some of the Gaullist faithful came to suspect that General de Gaulle might not be the person best equipped to manage affairs and to handle the free-for-all of politics, whose rules he had not fully mastered. Raymond Aron apparently thought so, when he declared to Claude Mauriac : 'It's the General's fault. He is only concerned with strategy and he neglects tactics. One cannot just keep on saying "no", especially on the Parliamentary scene'. And what can be said of this letter from Michel Debré to Georges Pompidou, as early as 21 April 1949? 'Gloomily prophetic', is Jean Lacouture's comment:

> For my part, I rather despair of events and of men. Where are we heading for? To some extent the General has tried to bring about the revolt of the real country against the legal state. But the legal state defends itself well ... . All the better, because the

rules are fixed. When you are up against a *régime*, any weapon will do. The General, justifiably, does not want to use them all – but in that case you are condemned to play on the outside of the *régime*, and that is something the General neither wants nor is interested in. Will we be able to break out of this circle? Yes, if there is a catastrophe; no, if there isn't. It is safer to presume that there won't be, in which case, I don't see any future; or rather I see only one of slow decline.[18]

There was no catastrophe, as we know, but there certainly was decline, dissidence among the ranks and disenchantment on the part of the leader. Even before the movement went into hibernation in 1953, its fate had been sealed in the spring and summer of 1952. When Soustelle abandoned the presidency of the parliamentary group, forty-one of his colleagues demanded to join the ranks of the majority government without imposing drastic conditions, and de Gaulle himself thought about 'letting history pass by'.[19] A year later, after a mediocre showing in the municipal elections, he withdrew the RPF from the electoral race on 6 May 1953:

It is more than ever in the public interest for the RPF, released from the parliamentary *impasse*, to organize itself and broaden its base throughout the country so as to accomplish its mission. This mission is to serve as an *avant-garde*, not in some cartel organised by the political parties to save their own hides, but in bringing the people together across the nation and across the social spectrum in order to change the evil *régime*. The opportunity to achieve this may come from some future consultation with the people held in different circumstances, when the climate has been radically altered. Alternatively, it may also come from a sudden shift in public opinion which, in the grips of anxiety, might lead the French to unite and the régime to become transformed. But alas, it is quite likely to come in the form of a serious upheaval, in which case the most pressing necessity would once again be the salvation of the country and of the state. The collapse of illusions is imminent. We must prepare our line of resort.[20]

---

[18]Lacouture, *De Gaulle*, Vol.2, pp.363–4. (This quotation is omitted from p.148 of the abridged English translation, *De Gaulle. The Ruler*, cited in footnote 2).
[19]De Gaulle, *Discours et messages. Dans l'attente*, p.536.
[20]De Gaulle, *Discours et messages. Dans l'attente*, p.582.

The moment of salvation

Here again the vision of disaster came to the fore, but this time with no political means available by which to try to avert it or put it to use. The real 'crossing of the desert' was beginning, and the period of latency was settling in. This could be clearly seen from de Gaulle's tone, which from now on displayed a mixture of anguish and contempt, threats and jocular insults hurled at the *'politichiens'* and even at the French themselves, whom he described as 'fools'. 'Of course, de Gaulle isn't in power, but we have killed off the régime', he was even said to have commented, with the horrific words of André Diethelm still echoing in the background in1953: 'We are not dead, because we can still destroy ... '. [21]

A sense of resentment had set in permanently, and neither the completion of the war memoirs, nor the walkabouts organized on his African trip or on his lightning visit to the Pacific islands, were enough to dispel it. He sensed all too keenly, to quote Jean Lacouture, that 'from the triumphalism of 1947 to the sense of catastrophe of 1953, a black cloud had been hovering over this ambiguous undertaking'.[22] His public aura had become tarnished, visitors became more infrequent, and the one-liners that he tried out on them, on the subject of Algeria or the survival of the 'system', revealed a bitter level of tunnel vision. How much worse could things get?

The experience of the RPF seemed to have laid to rest the idea of a popular *rassemblement* which had been a source of such strength for Gaullists. In the eyes of the left, it had accentuated the Bonapartist, Boulangiste and even 'Fascist' sides of the Gaullist movement and its leader. De Gaulle himself could probably not yet see what a wealth of militant devotion and of support among the Gaullist élite the RPF still had in reserve, nor the extent to which he would be able to draw on this wealth after 1958. For the time being, meditating on his failure and remembering the faces of friends he had visited in the provinces who had taught him about rural France, he seemed convinced that Gaullism and political parties were essentially incompatible. He had perhaps even resolved never again to wander along the paths of such an experience.

From that point on, the real rescue was to come from the vital event itself, suddenly validating the hero's principles, wiping out his failures and restoring his sagging stature. A faithful few soon sensed that the event in question would have to come from the direction of Algeria, or more precisely Algiers, and accordingly went into action both there and in Paris. The general expressed his New Year wishes for 1958 to one of

[21]Lacouture, *De Gaulle*, Vol. 2, p.398. (Only the first of these quotations is given on p.154 of *De Gaulle. The Ruler,*).
[22]Lacouture, *De Gaulle, The Ruler*, p.398.

them, Pierre Lefranc, in foreboding terms: 'I despair of our country as much as you do. It is simply that I doubt whether any message, in the present situation, could reverse the course of events. If the climate were to change, then yes, we should act. As for this new climate, let those who can begin preparing it immediately'.[23] Another of the elements of this change in the 'climate' was the gradual recovery of his popularity ratings in the surveys carried out by the *IFOP* – not a tidal wave by any means, but a faint surge which provided some consolation. In December 1955, only 1 per cent of the French hoped that de Gaulle would one day become president of the Council, but by July 1956 it was 9 per cent, and in January 1958 this rose to 13 per cent – still rather mediocre, but by then the general's popularity had finally outstripped that of Guy Mollet or Pierre Mendès-France. Between Algeria and the worries of the French people, events were stirring that would soon bring an end to the period of waiting.

---

[23]De Gaulle, *Lettres, Notes, et Carnets, 1951–1958*, p.343.

4

The Writing of Action in de Gaulle's War Memoirs

Robert Pickering

It is scarcely surprising that action should figure so predominantly in de Gaulle's *War Memoirs*, in view of its author's exemplary political and military career. But it is misleading to reduce the real literary significance of the notions of act and action in the work to the reconstitution of various military feats and their political consequences. To that 'certain idea of France' (p.9) which opens the memoirs there corresponds what one could call a 'certain idea of French', whose real meaning extends well beyond the masterly control of various prose techniques.[1] This mastery has been sufficiently studied for us to pass over the range of stylistic devices used by the writer, with the exception of those whose importance has either been neglected or which contribute in a pertinent way to the analytical perspective broached in this chapter.[2] As the progressive enactment of their very subject matter, the *War Memoirs* are highly significant in other

[1] Edition used: Charles de Gaulle, *Mémoires de guerre* (Plon, Paris, 1989). Although the abridged translation into English has been consulted (see Select Bibliography), and has occasionally guided the translation of quotations from the French original to be found in the text, these latter have by and large been translated anew. All page references to quotations are thus to the 1989 French edition.

[2] See particularly a special number of the review *Nord* (revue de critique et de création littéraires du Nord/Pas-de-Calais), 14 (1989), entitled 'De Gaulle écrivain – De Gaulle et les écrivains'. Also useful are F. Quesnoy, 'Le Style de Charles de Gaulle dans les "Mémoires de guerre" et les "Mémoires d'espoir"' (doctoral thesis, University of Paris IV [Sorbonne], 1987); Y. Le Hir, 'Les Appels électoraux du Général de Gaulle: étude de stylistique quantitative', in *Travaux de linguistique et de littérature*, 10/1, pp.141–70; J. Levron, *Dictionnaire commenté de l' oeuvre du Général de Gaulle* (Plon, Paris, 1975); *Le Vocabulaire du Général de Gaulle: une réflexion sur les méthodes en lexicologie. Actes du 2e colloque de lexicologie politique* (Klincksieck, Paris, 1982).

directions. If, for de Gaulle, to engage in action leads subsequently to writing, the latter is invested at the same time with an imperative of action, understood as the location and materialization, through the act of writing, of the structure and peculiarities of experience. It is this active principle of the text which calls for study, since it highlights the way in which de Gaulle turns to writing as the means to revivify and recreate the complex evolution of events defining an exceptional career – a recreation which, in a valid sense, creates those events precisely through the dynamic properties of writing.

Writing and a sense of vision

The *War Memoirs* demonstrate clearly that the fundamental components of de Gaulle's vision are perceived as given from the outset, since they must necessarily refer back to that 'certain idea of France' whose resonance grows consistently throughout the text. For both the memorialist, however, about to set pen to paper, and for the man of action engaging with a specific series of events, the deeper moral value of this vision of things remains to be explored and articulated, whether for an international readership or, perhaps more problematic still, for the French public itself. A discrepancy between a given initial vision and a project yet to be realized in prose thus begins to emerge, and provides the essential dynamic of a form of writing which, moving from one stage to the next, will be progressively composed as act. The unity and the conviction of a certain sense of identity, in which the vision of the man of action is embedded, must be created in and by writing. Even if the crucial prerequisite of a complete personal adherence to that vision is present from the opening lines of the text, its overall legitimacy in a general context of implementation and unification remains yet to be established. It should be noted that de Gaulle avoids the facile strategy of simply illustrating this evolution of events, looking back over the past in its comforting stability, and chooses instead to engage actively with all the shifting indeterminacy of a situation which is constantly presented as yet to be clarified, or fundamentally in progress.

The memorialist thus creates a tension between the given elements of his vision of things and the quest for their realization. The act of remembering events, fixed as historical fact, is modulated by the writing, which must act as vehicle in the quest for unity by instituting a parallel search for appropriate forms of composition and structuring. Hence the singularly dynamic framework of these memoirs, their perfectly organic tissue of insights but also of quandaries, of clarifications but also of uncertainty. The ordering of events and of the frequently secret or indeterminate causes which underpin them is at the same time that of writing itself, of the latter's operations and strategies which together define the functioning of the text. Far more than simply representing events, the writing enacts them, and substantiates their progression. A structural framework characterized by its dynamism constantly asserts its presence over any kind of static representation: the projected unity of the French must be effected as much by writing as by the sheer accumulation of descriptive affirmations, fixed in their historical solidity. In an extraordinary impetus towards composition, the writing imposes itself progressively in its generative force, thus creating its own internal coherence and autonomous status.

Vision and stylistic techniques

The vision which has to be communicated is therefore also a style which has to be created. Although the latter is grounded in previous publications, the *War Memoirs* have certain highly significant peculiarities. The presence of techniques such as anaphora or the repetition of certain syntactical elements has been studied before, but their active role in ordering thought has not been sufficiently highlighted. The repetition of the same word at the beginning of several sentences or clauses creates a network of accumulating relationships, whose stylistic effect is to explore all the possibilities or consequences of a given set of data. A memorandum sent by de Gaulle in January 1940 to the main personalities in government aims to convince them of five interlinked proposals, formulated, within the same sentence, by means of five repetitions of the relative pronoun *que*, which define both the independent status and the limits of each.[3] On other occasions, the repeated use of a specific group of words at the beginning of a sentence gives emphasis to a whole series of reflections, accentuating the latter's urgency or significance in an inexorable accumulation of facts, such as the impersonal construction *il est vrai que* (it is true that) whose extension to nearly an entire paragraph reiterates the lack of preparation or of properly professional training in the hastily constituted units serving under de Gaulle in May 1940.[4] The return to

[3]'J'adressai un mémorandum destiné à les convaincre que l'ennemi prendrait l'offensive ... ; que, de ce fait, notre front pouvait être, à tout moment, franchi; que ... nous risquions fort d'être anéantis; qu'il fallait décider ... la création de l'instrument voulu; que ... il était urgent de réunir ... des unités existantes' (*Mémoires de guerre*, p.31).
[4]'Il est vrai que, sur quelque 150 chars dont je dispose ... , 30 seulement sont du type B ... , et que le reste: Renault 35 n'a que des pièces courtes de 37 ... . Il est vrai que l' artillerie vient d'être constituée au moyen de détachements fournis par de multiples dépôts ... . Il est vrai qu'il n'y a pas, pour nous, de réseau-radio et que je ne puis commander qu' en dépêchant des motocyclistes ... . Il est vrai qu'il manque ... beaucoup des moyens de transport, d'entretien, de ravitaillement (que les unités) devraient, normalement, comporter. Cependant, il se dégage, déjà, de cet ensemble improvisé, une impression d'ardeur générale' (ibid., pp.40–1).

previously formulated elements is all the more effective since it is frequently suspended, towards the end of a given paragraph, by an adversative, whose presence makes relative the crushing accumulation of detail. Sometimes even this element of attenuation is lacking, a tendency which is usually reserved for moments of flagging hope, as, for example, during the rout in May 1940 and the distancing which is essential in order to take full measure of the enormous task ahead.[5] The recourse to syntactical repetition is still to be seen much later in the chronological order of events: at the 'cleansing' of power structures immediately subsequent to the Liberation (the so-called *épuration*), the text shows a similar desire to list and categorize all the component factors of a given situation, highlighting the latter's complexity in its minute detail, as in all its truth.[6]

This technique of repetition suggests the effort devoted in the *War Memoirs* towards ordering, classifying and weighing the mass of primary material formed by the detailed appraisal of hostilities and the attempts to rescue France from its predicament. What is particularly noteworthy here is above all the work of the mind itself, as it engages with the full complexity of its subject matter, which constantly threatens to escape any ordering and co-ordinating aspiration. The dynamism of the text can be seen even more clearly in the manipulation of certain temporal frames of reference. De Gaulle's use of the conditional and the future, as well as of the full play of expressive possibilities in the distinction between indicative and subjunctive moods, powerfully orientates the text towards that vision of activity in which the founding vision of the writing is embedded. Early in the writing can be located a tendency to imagine other possible types of action, to formulate strategies other than those actually implemented, a stylistic procedure which runs directly counter

---

[5]'Ce que je savais des hommes et des choses ne me laissait pas d'illusions sur les obstacles à surmonter. Il y aurait la puissance de l'ennemi ... . Il y aurait les difficultés morales et matérielles ... . Il y aurait la montagne des objections, imputations, calomnies ... . Il y aurait les entreprises dites "parallèles", mais en fait rivales et opposées ... .Il y aurait ... la volonté de dévoyer la résistance nationale vers le chaos révolutionnaire ... . Il y aurait, enfin, la tendance des grands Etats à profiter de notre affaiblissement' (ibid., pp.77–8).

[6]'Il faut, qu'en même temps, paraisse (la) justice (de l'Etat). Eu égard aux épreuves subies, la libération déclenchera, sans nul doute, une impulsion élémentaire de châtiment. Alors que des hommes et des femmes ... auront été ... fusillés, ... déportés ... , que des milliers de combattants ... auront été abattus sur place, que d'innombrables meurtres, incendies, pillages, brutalités, auront en outre été commis ... ; alors que ... maints journaux, revues ... auront prodigué les insultes à ceux qui se battent pour la France ... ; alors que ... certains auront étalé ... leur collaboration avec l'envahisseur, la fuite des Allemands risquera fort d'être le signal de sommaires et sanglantes revanches. Pourtant, en dépit de tout, nul particulier n'a le droit de punir les coupables. C' est là l'affaire de l'Etat' (ibid., p.449).

to the pressure simply to relate events in their apparent inevitability. What France 'might have done', were it not for a lack of will in military and governmental circles, becomes not just a constant of the text's overall objectives, but also a source of vitality, investing syntax with the energy of the mind's activity:

> During those difficult hours, I could not stop myself imagining what the mechanized army which I had so long dreamed about might have been able to do. Had it been there on that day, suddenly to open the way towards Guise, the advance of the Panzer divisions would have been halted, serious confusion caused in the German rear, and the northern group of (French) armies enabled to link up again with those of the centre and east.[7]

The play of imagination never remains, however, in a perspective of pure hypothesis. It is here that the guiding force of the vision in the opening lines of the work can be felt: at the most decisive moments of the overall enterprise, a military or political strategy does not need to be set in place, since it has already been forcefully affirmed. From the outset, certain points of reference capable of realizing a potential course of action, even if this course is not known when the writing begins, suggest its primary directions, whether in the framework of criticism levelled at governmental inconsistency, or in that of other proposed guidelines of action, other principles of preparation and implementation.

An alternating rhythm of composition is thus set up in the first pages of the *Memoirs*, functioning between, on the one hand, the affirmation of values felt to be secure – 'I intend to keep up hope' (*'j'entends garder l'espérance'*), 'the Empire is there ... the fleet is there ... the people are there ... the world is there' (pp.46–7), and, on the other, the exploration of strategies of action in which the initiative lost in events is free to develop. The conditional tense and the subjunctive mood, which are by definition the verbal vehicles for qualification or indecisiveness, are often invested with a paradoxical sense of certainty. 'To overcome the disaster, (General Weygand) would have had to renew himself'; 'Despite everything, I am convinced that in other times, Marshal Pétain would not have consented to don the purple in the midst of national collapse'; 'Had France between the wars had at its head a capable state ... , what destiny would have been ours!'. Far from limiting themselves to the expression of regret or of sterile nostalgia, such remarks sketch in the shadowy

[7]'Au cours de ces heures difficiles, je ne puis m'empêcher d'imaginer ce qu'eût pu faire l'armée mécanique dont j'avais si longtemps rêvé. Qu'elle eût été là, ce jour-là, pour déboucher soudain vers Guise, l'avance des Panzerdivisions était arrêté du coup, un trouble grave jeté dans leurs arrières, le groupe d'armées du Nord en mesure de se ressouder à ceux de Centre et de l'Est' (ibid., p.41).

virtuality of another state of things, both unattainable and yet the vital dynamic of real acts which take root in it.[8]

The same is true of the role assumed by the future, which can have the force of reality, and less the status of tentative projection, more or less distanced in time. Such is the case with Mandel's remark to de Gaulle in June 1940, 'You will have a great duty to fulfil, General' (*'vous aurez de grands devoirs a remplir'*,'p.66), or with the conviction, formed already in 1941, of an allied landing in France, 'When one day we land on French soil proper' (*'Quand nous débarquerons, un jour, sur le sol français proprement dit'*,' p.175). If the future can be subject to doubt ('For [France], what is at stake is not only the expulsion of the enemy from her territory, it is also her future as a nation and a state', p.273), the uncertainty concerns the form of national sovereignty that victory will bring, not the possibility of the latter's realization.

The numerous questions which appear in the text are also a part of the modification which is brought to bear on the traditional use of grammatical models. Contrary to its conventional use, the rhetorical question is often far removed from any attempt to dramatize the narrative, or to persuade the reader. It is more usually bent towards indicating values which are at stake, or towards sounding in advance the possibilities and the risks of action:

> But the war continues. It remains to be won. What will be the price of the outcome? What ruins will be added to our ruins? What new losses will decimate our soldiers? What moral and physical hardships will the French who are prisoners of war still have to suffer? How many of our deportees will return ... ? Finally, in what state will our people emerge, and in the midst of what kind of world?[9]

Above all, it should be stressed that such a series of questions in no way slows the progression of the text. On the contrary, the interrogative tone maintains the rhythm of the statements, and foreshadows the importance of considerations which will only figure later in the writing. By its contextual role, the questioning thus complements the process of

[8]'Pour faire tête au malheur, il eût fallu que (General Weygand) se renouvelât' (p.48); 'Malgré tout, je suis convaincu qu'en d'autres temps, le maréchal Pétain n'aurait pas consenti à revêtir la pourpre dans l'abandon national' (p.68); 'Que la France, entre les deux guerres, eût eu à sa tête un Etat capable ... , quel destin était le nôtre!' (ibid., p.545).
[9]'Mais la guerre continue. Il reste à gagner. De quel prix ... faudra-t-il payer le résultat? Quelles ruines s'ajouteront à nos ruines? Quelles pertes nouvelles décimeront nos soldats? Quelles peines morales et physiques auront à subir encore les Français prisonnniers de guerre? Combien reviendront parmi nos déportés ... ? Finalement, dans quel état se retrouvera notre peuple et au milieu de quel univers?' (ibid., p.584)

spatialization and of differentiation which reaffirms values at the very moment of their apparent undermining, and works in close conjunction with the particularities of temporal and modal usage.

The quest for form

The opening of the text, the proliferation of its levels of functioning and the interpretative sonority with which it is imbued, raise the writing to the status of a work perceived in its becoming. But form has to be circumscribed, even if the vision with which the writing is impregnated constantly presides over its elaboration. This formative activity through the written word is closely linked to that, equally generative, of the spoken one: the writer interacts with the leader who, as early as 18th June 1940, speaks 'in the name of France' (p.144). 'On 18 June, when I broadcast for the first time in my life and imagined, with a certain sense of dizziness, those who were listening, I discovered what a part radio propaganda was going to play in our undertaking': through radio broadcasts speaking and writing come together in a concerted thrust towards communication and persuasion.[10]

Given that the spoken and the written word function in such close harmony, the structure which they require, with its internal divisions and organizational criteria, must be sufficiently flexible to act as vehicle for the global ambition which is the writing's point of departure. In the face of the uncertainties of strategy, of the deviations and about-turns in variable political considerations, a framework must be found, sufficiently flexible to accommodate the apparent inconsistencies of improvisation, yet also to express the firmness of a particular vision, characterized by its finality and its intransigence. The absolute priority given to what is 'in conformity with the interests of France' (p.172), and the very nature of politics which, in de Gaulle's view, is defined as 'action in the service of a strong and simple idea' (p.228), must necessarily come to terms with contexts in which the realities of power, be they invested in German, Vichy, Free French or even British and American interests, are far less clearly defined.

The search for a satisfactory structure, able to co-ordinate a composite view formed of extremely diverse data, is therefore linked to the very nature of the conflict – to the latter's necessities, constraints, expedients and constant risks of compromise, sometimes also to the exceptional possibilities of freedom in decisive action which the radical fragmentation of national identity has at least the merit of opening up.

---

[10]'Le 18 juin, parlant à la radio pour la première fois de ma vie et imaginant, non sans vertige, celles et ceux qui étaient à l'écoute, je découvrais quel rôle allait jouer dans notre entreprise la propagande par les ondes' (ibid., p.139).

The problematic of the search for form

One of the primary factors which presides over the evolution of, and hence the deepest functional levels operative in, the writing, is certainly the oscillation between admiration of, and critical reserve towards, the British. The variations in attitude are sometimes starkly represented: in the space of three pages (208–10), an icy response (in reaction to Churchill's refusal to meet de Gaulle, regarding fundamental differences of approach to Syria and to the Lebanon) can give way to the reverse (recognition by the British government of the constitution of the Syrian and Lebanese Republics), without giving the impression of an incoherence in events. London acquires the status of a stabilizing point of reference, 'communications centre and capital of the war' (p.188), whose interests remain indissolubly linked to those of the Free French. Organized around this axis, the writing follows the occasionally brutal acceleration of events, or, on the contrary, the paralysis of action in equivocation and seemingly endless postponement.

What would at first sight appear to be the rather unco-ordinated rhythms of the writing are in fact finely attuned to the overlapping of events, political considerations and the question of a legitimate identity for the Free French. Our interpretation of certain syntactic tendencies, already noted, can be clarified in this perspective. The lengthy sentences, with their numerous clauses, can be replaced with much shorter and more energetic declarations ('We had to play a tight game', 'It was time to react'), which truncate the elaboration of political complexities and reaffirm the dynamism of action.[11] At other moments, like those concerning the Normandy landings and the victories in Italy, the writing can be made to accelerate by omitting the auxiliary and retaining only an accumulation of past participles.[12] On the occasion of de Gaulle's visit to Bayeux, the syntax again mimes the turn of events, either by giving prominence to short, lapidary sentences,[13] or by accumulating nouns to portray the enthusiasm of the crowds.[14] From these stylistic variations there emerges a progressive integration of de Gaulle with the identity of a particular undertaking. Hence, too, the increasing frequency in the use of a particular device which pushes this integration to ever greater

---

[11]'Il nous fallait jouer serré' (ibid., p.213); 'Il était temps de réagir' (ibid., p.216).

[12]'Le succès militaire produisant ses effets, le roi Victor-Emmanuel a transmis ses pouvoirs à son fils, Badoglio donnné sa démission, Bonomi formé, à Salerne, le nouveau gouvernement' (ibid., p.504).

[13]'Sortant des maisons, ils me font cortège au milieu d'une extraordinaire émotion. Les enfants m'entourent. Les femmes sourient et sanglotent. Les hommes me tendent les mains' (ibid., p.502).

[14]'Nous allons ainsi, tous ensemble, bouleversés et fraternels, sentant la joie, la fierté, l'espérance nationales remonter du fond des abîmes' (ibid., p.502).

lengths: a tendency to replace the normally directive 'self' of the narration by a mode of representation in the third person, the 'de Gaulle' who thinks, judges and acts. Thus is engendered, through the effacement of the first person, a play of points of view which might at first disconcert the reader, but which is certainly not pretentious or manipulative. For the 'self' can itself be scrutinized and commented upon, as if the principle of rhythmic alternation demanded from time to time an appraisal of the narrator's performance – a process which returns so regularly, and with such increasing intensity, that it soon becomes one of the text's primary representational modes.[15]

A second problematical oscillation which is strongly imposed on the structural development of the writing concerns the difference between fragmentation and consolidation. A dialectical relationship is powerfully enacted at the heart of all the related activities, and participates in the structural evolution of the writing. 'Our forces ... , however reduced and dispersed they were and although we could only construct them out of bits and pieces, now formed a coherent whole which was continuously consolidated' (p.249): the text frequently reads as if it were the metaphorical transposition of a process which is taking place, that of a unification which is progressively being realized in the complex interaction of men and of their beliefs. The quest for united action is visible on several levels, but nowhere is it present with greater force than in the imperative of co-ordinating metropolitan resistance, in the wish to establish 'some unity in the political action within France, ... as in the military action' (p.242). Such frequently used terms as *'relier'*('link', p.243), *'entrer dans l'unité nationale'*('return to the unity of the nation', p.240) and *'former un tout'*('form a whole', p.236) give the tone of a form of writing bent towards reunification, all the more dynamic since composed of a multitude of individual events, perceived in their simultaneity, yet to be co-ordinated into a meaningful whole.

De Gaulle can turn to retrospection, in the attempt to implement this vast unifying ambition. The reader happens upon mini-prefigurations of future events (anticipation of the Russian victories, p.204, or foretelling of the destiny of Jean Moulin, p.241). But in general, the future of the war, which by definition is known at the time of writing, is regularly

---

[15]Examples of this tendency, ibid., pp.227, 230, 250, 408 ('ce de Gaulle'), 612, 691, 836 ('Je ne puis me dissimuler que mon projet va heurter de front les prétentions des partis. Tel ou tel d' entre eux ... ne se résout pas encore à s'opposer à de Gaulle' – in this example, within the space of two sentences, the 'self' is emptied from the narration, dispossessed to the benefit of the third person which will dominate the rest of the paragraph, in an act of self-effacement which conforms generally with the self's eclipse towards the end of the text, as de Gaulle's wishes are submerged in the gathering clamour of the political parties).

dramatized and evoked in its original uncertainty.[16] The quest for French identity cannot give the impression of being known in advance, and must therefore remain attuned to the unforeseeable nature of an immersion in the global situation. Moreover, the writing imposes its own laws in the progressive recreation of events, demanding respect of the strategies and of the constant mobility of a given set of military or political circumstances. Beyond the finality presiding over its own evolution, it must in particular engender the feeling of the variability in Franco-British relations, and convey the vigour of efforts devoted by de Gaulle to dispelling mysteries, clarifying misunderstandings and circumventing silence.[17]

Thus the essential part of the effort devoted to the operations of writing, working in parallel with those of memory, has to be materialized with a constant eye to structure and unification, in which all the resources of language are actively engaged. This process is quite different from the unifying action of de Gaulle's 'self', even if the *je* imposes itself everywhere on the vicissitudes of military and political developments. At the moment when these memoirs begin, the historical outcome of events is well known. Another struggle now unfolds, that of the mobilization of language's own most effective powers of performance, of its resources of thematic concentration and interpretative potential. A problematical identity is slowly crystallized, without reducing the proliferation of personalities, hopes and opinions which constitute its singular specificity. A remarkable complementarity grows progressively between the identity of a movement and the identity of language itself: the success of the latter can be measured in the threats and traps which, on nearly every page, are shown to endanger the former. The battle engaged with Vichy to represent France, lack of consideration or consultation emanating from the British and from the Americans, the relationship with the enemy and the long conflict for an *'autorité connue, sinon reconnue'*('an authority which was visible, if not recognized', p.269) clearly to emerge, elevating the Free French above the status of unofficial auxiliaries,[18] are all essential points

[16]'En tenant ce langage, je jouais moins sur le présent, qui m'offrait peu de moyens de soutenir la querelle, que sur l'avenir où la France, peut-être, aurait de quoi la reprendre, pourvu que ceux qui parlaient en son nom eussent la fermeté voulue pour refuser l' abandon' (ibid., p.294).

[17]The pages devoted to the controversy created by British operations in North Africa and in Madagascar are highly significant in this respect (ibid., pp.295–7): 'Tous ceux qui, chez eux, s'occupaient des préparatifs continuaient d'observer un silence absolu. Mais, si cette conjuration du secret nous semblait désobligeante, elle était, de surcroît, inutile. Car, d'Amérique, d'Angleterre, de France, affluaient des renseignements ... . Tout annonçait de grands desseins qui ne visaient point l'Europe ... . Tout était clair, désormais. ... Tout en animant ainsi la controverse, je m'appliquais à éclaircir les affaires à l'intérieur du pays'.

[18]For example, the German attitude towards the French prisoners at Bir-Hakeim ('Les Français blancs et de couleur ... n'appartenant pas à une armée régulière, subiront les lois de la guerre et seront exécutés', ibid., p.266); de Gaulle's immediate reaction ('à

of reference which mark the long movement towards official recognition, and which constantly threaten the impetus of its evolution.

The strategies and the stakes of writing

To be able to act as vehicle for the operations of a fighting entity, formed of numerous isolated contributions which are to be seen not just on the level of attitudes but also on the strictly syntactic level of pronominal displacement, particularly the concomitance of *je/il* (I/he) and its subsequent shift into a collective *nous* (we), the writing must echo the 'organizational plan' (p.249) which is one of the general's primary preoccupations.[19] The necessity of clearly defined goals has important repercussions on the organization of the narrative, creating its own obligations in structuring and form, its own moments of intensity and of release.[20] The act of writing is increasingly presented as an act of co-ordination, of constant realignment and modification, characterized by its fluidity. To 'outline' and 'formulate' the 'immense battle of communications ... in all its fluctuations' (p.255) become essential strategic imperatives in the realization of a form of writing which must necessarily be hinged on the 'hard logic of events' (p.339).

This strategy is, above all, closely linked to the play of overlapping timescales. 'Winter approaches. Everything suggests that it will be the last before the final trial of arms. But what form of power will then be established in Paris? ... Everyone knows that France will reappear. Everyone wonders what she will be. ... But it is the resistance which is today providing the war effort and which bears the hope of renewal' (p.421): the writing must project the uncertain perspectives of a none the less known future, and must situate it in relation to present difficulties, all the while maintaining the impetus of a progressing continuity

---

son profond regret il se verrait obligé d'infliger le même sort aux prisonniers allemands', ibid., pp.266–7); and the subsequent German guarantee that 'Les soldats du Général de Gaulle seront traités comme des soldats', bear clear testimony to the effort of identification of which the text charts the long and difficult course, crowned with success at Bir-Hakeim, long before official recognition by the Allies ('Quant aux alliés, il leur fallait se résigner à voir la France en guerre conduite par un gouvernement français').

[19]Ibid., p.250 is characteristic of this phenomenon of pronominal slippage. In the space of a few lines, a subjective mode of portrayal ('En 1940, j'ai créé leur école ["cadets de la France libre"]' turns to an objective one ('Rien ne réconforte autant le chef des Français Libres que le contact de cette jeunesse'), before finally being integrated in the dynamism of a collective force ('c'est à partir des ports anglais que la plupart de nos forces navales prennent part ... à la bataille des communications').

[20]The moments of relative calm, in which figure members of the general's family and some details of private life, have all the more impact for being scarce, such as the lull ('Je revois ma vie, en ce temps', ibid., p.247) which ushers in two short paragraphs before being replaced by the trepidating rhythm of official duties.

and reflecting as closely as possible the mobile trajectory which under-pins the inexorable march of events. For the conviction that *'notre Dame la France'* ('our lady France') will one day be victorious must itself con-stantly be respected. Retrospection thus has the role of modulating the distance between the unforeseeable nature of events and the firm belief in 'the victory of France' (p.420). Retrospective appraisal has nothing to it of simple clarification, aiming to justify a given attitude or line of con-duct. In the course of the work this retrospection becomes a technique of capital importance in a vision which, despite the solidity of its found-ing convictions, must come to terms with the evolution of the war. In this constant process of adaptation, conceptions of the future will, in ef-fect, be related increasingly to France's destiny after liberation, adding in this way to the dynamism of these 'war memoirs' by prefiguring those of peace. Considerations bearing on a post-Liberation France become more and more frequent, and focus on the very place which de Gaulle might occupy in a newly constituted government.

The play of retrospection can be seen not just in relation to the memorialist's present circumstances of composing the text, but also in relation to events previously related. Thus General Giraud's retirement, figuring on p.440 of the text, is followed on p.519 by a reference to his attitude towards American policies when he was still actively engaged in the conflict, as by other significant allusions (pp.528, 531 and 880) made at moments when he has long since withdrawn from the political and military fray. Such returns to the past counterbalance the dominant lin-earity of the prose, by suggesting rather the simultaneity of events in a context which is less temporal than spatial. The same is true of the immense activity caused by the Allied landings in Normandy (pp.501–3), the culminating point of a huge logistical and tactical effort which we would normally be expecting to dominate the narrative at the expense of all else. The context of the landings is followed by de Gaulle's visit to Italy (pp.504–6), an episode which makes relative the importance of met-ropolitan France by the parallel established with other fronts, while all the time remaining at the heart of the hopes and preoccupations of Free France's military action.

For it is imperative that all strategic preliminaries be effected before approaching the *'terrain plus meuble'* ('the more fluid terrain') and the *'air moins pur'* ('less pure air') of France itself, rife with rumour and subjected constantly to the claims and counterclaims of propaganda. In terms of the global evolution of the text, analysis of metropolitan France cannot figure in the writing before the various mechanisms which govern the composition are put in place. This order of events is, of course, also dictated by purely pragmatic and chronological considerations: by the nature of things, the movement towards liberation is strongest at first on the periphery, since metropolitan resistance is engendered in isolation and is subject to increasingly intense decimation. But the fact remains that the writing plays an integral role in the constitution of an historical movement, thereby acquiring a status of autonomy. To be capable of embracing the full complexity of France and its seething activity, the text must first be able to master the diversity of its own structural virtualities and modes of composition. The movement towards France's unity, in the widest sense of the term, is simultaneously that which, constantly struggling with the tensions of the writing's texture and the multiple pressures of an immense scenario, must strenuously counteract the possibility of disintegration. The administrative bodies of the Council of Liberation, composed of 'bits' and 'pieces' (p.447), are the figurative projection of the work in progress, even if the latter remains steadfastly embedded in, and guided by, the ardent faith of the beginning.

In this way, we are invited to read the text as a metaphor of its own functioning, by means of its procedures and techniques of planning, coordination and distribution. A statement such as 'If politics requires an impetus which elevates it, it is also only the art of possiblities' articulates, beyond its apparent transparency, not just the directions but also the mechanisms of the writing, that 'art of possibilities' which necessitates being taken in hand, without losing the dynamism at its core.[21] This depth of the text, where statement and the act of stating constantly interact and invigorate one another, finds its most intense point of concentration in the dual status of 'France', which is both supreme symbol, the goal to be attained in the finality of the act of writing, and the point of convergence of literally global efforts, whose integral components rightfully claim to be recognized. In the progression towards metropolitan France, composed of contributions from the entire Empire, there is affirmed the strategic relationship between centre and periphery which has presided over all the actions of the Free French movement, a relationship of direct dependence which legitimizes the whole. What occurs on the periphery of events permanently underscores and supports what happens at the centre of things, and, to a certain degree, vice versa (reports by intermediaries of what is really taking place in France, or the efforts of central forces to aid the periphery, particularly at the time of the Normandy landings).

The image used by de Gaulle of the cogs ('*rouages*', p.543) of a living machine, motivated by a single goal, exteriorizes the power of this fundamental strategic principle. The necessity of co-ordinating effort, as well as the quest for a solidarity of action and interaction in which all constituent elements would be in free communication, characterizes a narrative in which 'the struggle of France forms a whole' (p.549). A deep structural logic influences the organization of the text's elaboration

---

[21]'S'il faut à la politique un élan qui la soulève, elle ne saurait être autre chose que l'art des possibilités' (ibid., p.447).

in the chapter entitled *'Combat'*, which can be placed in a constant oscillation between the theatre of metropolitan operations broached in Normandy, the exploits of the Resistance in France and the central contribution in Italy and in Indochina of the military forces of the Provisional Government of the Republic. 'We knew full well that the problem of Indochina ... would only be settled in Paris' (p.558): the struggle for the periphery is simultaneously that for the centre. Until the end of the writing, this interaction will remain the dominant structuring principle, the centre being defined as much in relation to what it is not as in relation to core convictions situated over and above the numerous currents and conflicting tendencies generated beyond it.

But for a protracted period of time, the 'centre' cannot but remain unstable. Are we invited to interpret it as Paris, in which nothing remains but the nostalgia for a lost sovereignty? Vichy, which illegitimately, in de Gaulle's view, claims to be the central focus? London, the necessary administrative centre for a movement constantly struggling to safeguard its independence? The chapter entitled *'Paris'* unequivocally decides the question, and Pétain's final attempt at negotiation provokes de Gaulle's definitive declaration of sovereign status for the Free French.[22] But once identity and unity have been affirmed in their legitimizing central location, the text, in a final, supreme irony, begins to change direction back to the problematics of concentration and dispersion, in which it was originally engendered.

From the logic of events to the logic of writing

In the last section of the great structural triptych, *'Le Salut 1944–1946'* ('Salvation 1944–1946'), the liberation of the homeland and the unity which it implies are increasingly overtaken by what de Gaulle calls the 'rising tide of complacency' (p.726), by the risks of fragmentation of that very 'French unanimity' (p.733) which military action had forged. All means are valid in order to stem this evolution, notably the effort devoted to economic revival and the inclusion of communists in the government, to promote a 'unitary politics' (p.696). But the coming of peace alters the bases of action, and signals a change of vital importance to the narration. Churchill's electoral defeat in July 1945 is seen to show clearly the new direction of events: if in England 'public opinion and politics despoiled the psychology of union' (pp.799–800), post-war difficulties will not be long in emerging for de Gaulle either, difficulties which, by their very nature, arise from newly-won freedom of expression and the right to political difference. A number of factors amplify the growing dispersive

[22]'C'est moi qui détiens la légitimité. C'est en son nom que je puis appeler la nation à la guerre et à l'unité, imposer l'ordre, la loi, la justice, exiger au-dehors le respect des droits de la France. Dans ce domaine, je ne saurais le moins du monde renoncer, ni même transiger' (ibid., p.593).

tendencies, which can be perceived both externally to France (the impractical dream of a federation of the German regions, the problematical conception of a possible European unity in which old tensions inevitably resurface, or the cracks in the façade of an organization purporting to represent the 'United Nations'), and in differences internal to the French political context.

The growing incompatibility between the varied, even partisan, nature of the political parties and de Gaulle's view of the state soon brings to a conclusion the war memoirs. For the structural distribution and evolution of the writing have functioned to this point according to the inner logic generated by a particular rhythmic co-ordination of attitudes and actions. When the war reaches its inevitable outcome, the act of remembering and of narrating must also draw to a close, or else change mode and objectives in the elaboration of other memoirs, those precisely of 'hope'. Up to this point the writing has been in perfect accord with the march of events, with the imperatives of unification and of the affirmation of an identity which have presided over all its areas of functioning – particularly that of the problematics of centre and periphery, crystallizing the global vocation of France. These creative tensions are progressively neutralized, as the past catches up with the present. De Gaulle can now highlight the *'50 million de tonnes'* (p.833) of German coal which 'are being' transferred to France (*'que nous sommes en train d'obtenir'*), or point to the petroleum research organization which 'we have just' created (*'que nous venons d'instituer'*), as the actualizing dynamism of related events is incorporated in the present rhythms of the writing's elaboration. The varied temporal discrepancies which have inhabited the text to this point now fade and disappear in the act of thinking, of living and of putting pen to paper.

The narration of the past thus merges with the immediacy of the problems confronting France. But this temporal concordance is acquired at the very moment when the state 'divides against itself'(p.833) and, in de Gaulle's view, returns to the mediocrity of its former ways. The very foundation of the writing cannot admit that things could be otherwise. Quoting Buffon, for whom 'style only exists by order and movement' (*'il n'est de style que par l'ordre et le mouvement'*, p.687), the text refers to a relationship of necessity and of intimate concordance between events and the form which they assume, an overlapping which demands that the writing stops, as the impetus generated in the moving trajectory of a personal destiny, linked to that of the entire nation, is slowly dissipated. The man of action, in the face of what he sees to be the inadequacies of the emerging political forces, is strongly tempted to reinvigorate that trajectory.[23] But this possibility runs against the logic which had led de Gaulle

---

[23]On this point, de Gaulle is customarily forthright: 'je constate qu'aucune des formations politiques n'est en mesure d'assurer la conduite du pays et de l'Etat' (ibid., p.835).

to power in the first place, that 'psychology of union' which had been constituted in the face of a common enemy, and which can only disintegrate subsequently under the effect of entirely new political imperatives.

The same is true of the writing itself, in which order cannot be consecrated, or removed totally from the presence of any destabilizing undercurrents. The mode of textual elaboration adopted can only carry the narration further if it turns its back on the representational fidelity with which it is so deeply imbued. Having become the memoirs of peace, those of war must necessarily be dislocated as the voices of freedom reassert themselves. Moreover, the closing pages tend to refer us back to a form of legitimacy located in the past, as the existence of the text enters a period of reprieve in which the future is not engaged. The status of past hostilities is confirmed as the generative point of reference for the memorialist's activity. At the end, the future definitively loses the paradoxical reality and substance with which it was invested for most of the writing, an evolution which clearly points to the proximity of a conclusion. The 'nests of intrigue' (p.870) which complicate the referendum and the 'precarious' (p.874) exercise of power increasingly out of step with reality, cast their shadow over an unpredictable and even 'regrettable' (p.876) future, confirming in a striking way the modifications which have taken place in the elaboration of the text.

The text and its becoming

Nothing would be farther from the truth than to see in this evolution the flagging of inspiration, or a dubious introversion in the face of new difficulties. The presence of the past, for example, is not limited to the past which is lived by the memorialist. It testifies to a breadth of culture which is capable of establishing pertinent links between an isolated, personal destiny and the wealth of an unequalled literary heritage. Quotations taken from Valéry,[24] Hugo,[25] Chateaubriand,[26] Chamfort,[27] Vercors,[28] Byron,[29] Clemenceau,[30] Lewis Carroll,[31] Goethe[32] and Buffon, to cite only

---

[24]'Je citais Paul Valéry: "On verra se développer les entreprises d'hommes choisis, agissant par équipes, produisant en quelques instants, à une heure, dans un lieu imprévus des événements écrasants"'(ibid., p.15).

[25]'Le lendemain, Aymeri prit la ville' (ibid., p.118).

[26]'Si rudes que fussent les réalités, peut-être pourrais-je les maîtriser, puisqu' il m'était possible, suivant le mot de Chateaubriand, "d'y mener les Français par les songes"' (ibid., p.128).

[27]'Citant le mot de Chamfort: "Les raisonnables ont duré. Les passionnés ont vécu", j'évoque les deux années que la France Libre vient de parcourir' (ibid., p.268).

[28]'(La France) glissera du "silence de la mer" à l'asthénie définitive, de la servitude imposée par l'ennemi à la subordination par rapport aux alliés'(ibid., p.274).

[29]'L'Italie, devenue de nouveau, suivant le mot de Byron, "la triste mère d'un empire mort" ... , prenait le chemin de la rupture avec le Reich allemand' (ibid., p.403).

the *War Memoirs* , bear witness to the living presence in the texture of the writing of a deep cultural rooting. Although no explicit references can be found here to the writing and to the example of Péguy, a central figure in de Gaulle's experience, the last pages devoted to a depiction of Champagne owe much to the inspiration stemming from Péguy's mysticism, particularly to the latter's intermingling of spiritual revival and a profound sense of belonging to the homeland.

Another indication of this singular awareness of the literary past whose patrimony must also be safeguarded, can be found in the lexical resonance which manifests itself in a Cornelian perspective, present in accumulating references to notions of *'gloire'*[33], *'grandeur'*, *'destin'* and *'morale'*, as well as in the redemptive value of the sword (*'épée'*), a recurring image of vengeance but also of honour. The influence of the classical authors can also be seen in contexts which are in no way limited to the sole characteristics of syntactic or grammatical construction. The memoirs reveal a remarkably talented portraitist, and a feeling for detail which can sketch a character with the economy of means characterizing, for example, *Les Caractères* of La Bruyère. A similar mastery of technical means can be seen in the taste for descriptive precision, heightened occasionally by a considerable capacity for comic verve. The pages devoted to the difficult negotiations with Stalin, and emphasizing, precisely, the 'abyss which, for the Soviet world, separates words and deeds', (p.675), are exemplary in this perspective. Another literary parallel worthy of study can be perceived in this eminently active form of writing with what Valéry describes as the energy of the *'actes du discours'* ('action of speech', p.31) in Bossuet, for whom the act of preaching held that same power of the written and the spoken word that we have seen in de Gaulle, a power based on a comparably active structure which is both fixed and flexible.[34]

With this past and its rich cultural impregnation there corresponds a future which, despite its precarious nature, remains turned towards the possible. In the last pages, de Gaulle takes care to 'remain above circumstances' (p.880) and, marking his distance from Churchill, to 'leave events

[30]'Il faut que nos combattants ... aient sans délai la preuve que les coupables ont à répondre de leurs actes. Je le déclare à la tribune de l'Assemblée consultative en citant Georges Clemenceau: "La guerre! Rien que la guerre! La justice passe! Le pays connaîtra qu'il est défendu"' (ibid., p.451); 'S'il est vrai, d'après Clemenceau, que "la pire souffrance de l' âme est le froid", on comprend que l'atmosphère dans laquelle j'aurai à me mouvoir ... me sera chaque jour plus pénible' (ibid., p.839).

[31]'A vrai dire, les intentions du Président me paraissent du même ordre que les rêves d'Alice au pays des merveilles' (ibid., p.485).

[32]'Tandis que l' ennemi fuyait et que Vichy s'anéantissait, (les résistants) avaient été tentés de dire, comme le Faust de Goethe: "Instant! arrête-toi. Tu es si beau!"' (ibid., p.636).

[33]It is to be noted that one of the references to 'gloire' takes the form of the classical alexandrine in a complete sentence('Ce fut votre rôle et ce sera votre gloire', ibid., p.701).

[34]P.Valéry, *Oeuvres* (Paris, Gallimard, 1957), Vol. 1, pp.498–9.

before they leave me' (*'quitter les choses avant qu'elles ne me quittent'*, p.867). The status of the leader 'standing apart' (*'tenu à l'écart'*, p.883) is thereby kept intact, projecting a personality situated above the petty turmoil of everyday circumstances, the final recourse in any situation of real threat or of bitter national discord.[35] If the logic in which these war memoirs are embedded finally takes the upper hand, it nevertheless prefigures, through the action of its very components, the disintegration of that rare 'period without anguish' (p.883) which had temporarily intervened in the affairs of the nation. The interrogative tone of the concluding pages, taking up again the former process whereby the text was generated and developed, but invested now with a hint of anguish, would seem to cast a shadow over the realization of any future elaboration.[36] But there is, paradoxically, nothing uncertain or unpredictable in the possibility of the writing's regeneration. For the internal logic demanding that the text be interrupted at this point will necessitate no less the revival of the act of remembering and of the latter's materialization in the written word.

Hence a conclusion to the work which proves to be all the more definitive since it contains simultaneously the promise of regeneration, of an irrepressible 'to be continued' which will not be long in coming. The final lines tend, moreover, to prefigure this continuation, in, for example, various 'ideas prepared for the future' (*'idées faites pour l' avenir'*) articulated from 'many platforms' (p.884), and in the successful attempts to 'fuel the flame' (*'entretenir la flamme'*) of a discourse which is as generative as it is galvanizing. The end leaves us in no doubt of the cyclical return of a deep-rooted malaise, moving inexorably towards future crises, of the 'inevitable shock' (*'inévitable secousse'*) that the mechanism of the writing's internal logic carries within it.

It is also highly significant that the conclusion should return to the sources of that logic, by referring again in an apparently modified, but in fact strictly identical, context to the connection between centre and periphery. For the distancing from the exercise of political power is finally held to be a paradoxical removal towards the centre of things, a development which can be perceived on a number of profoundly concomitant levels. As de Gaulle writes, 'At the moment of finishing this

[35]'Dans le chef tenu à l'écart, on continuait de voir une sorte de détenteur désigné de la souveraineté, un recours choisi d'avance. On concevait que cette légitimité restât latente au cours d'une période sans angoisse. Mais on savait qu'elle s'imposerait, par consentement général, dès lors que le pays courrait le risque d'être, encore une fois, déchiré et menacé' (*Mémoires de guerre*, p.883).

[36]'Ce peuple, sous les témoignages émouvants qu'il me prodigue mais qui expriment sa détresse autant que son sentiment, n'est-il pas las, désabusé, divisé? Ces vastes entreprises, cette action vigoureuse, ces fortes institutions, que je propose à son effort, ne dépassent-elles pas ses moyens et ses désirs? Et moi, ai-je la capacité, l'habileté, l'éloquence, nécessaires pour le galvaniser, dès lors que tout s' aplatit?' (ibid., p.837).

book, I feel the same countless hearts turning towards my simple house'.[37] The context of distance becomes the focal point for reflection, a stabilizing point of reference towards which the nation's untold hopes and its ineradicable sense of unease seem to converge. The same is true of the serenity and the comfort which are afforded by close contact with provincial France, by the latter's reassuring way of life, regulated by the rhythm of the seasons and of age-old customs or beliefs. The last pages of the text bespeak an atmosphere of calmness and an awareness of the positive values of silence, the more effectively to highlight the importance of what is intuitively felt to be, in Colombey, a return to the very sources of the self's identity. The strength of this experience prompts the comment that 'henceforth the future belongs to me', a perception which can be measured in its full plenitude when the fulcrum of human enterprise attained in Colombey is again finally confirmed as activating the most distant points of man's endeavours, co-ordinating them in a totality which contains in it the promise of 'renewal' (p.886). Rousseau and Chateaubriand alone, perhaps, can equal the intensity of emotional identification between man and nature, achieved when the clamour of action is finally stilled. This action, above all, is affirmed yet again as being consubstantial with the principle of active generation at the writing's source. For the end of the work, closing the narrative in the perenniality of a particular conception of history, prefigures the rebirth of a vital dynamism, which continues to live in the reader's imagination through the very silence of the end of utterance.

---

[37]'Au moment d'achever ce livre, je sens, autant que jamais, d' innombrables sollicitudes se tourner vers une simple maison' (ibid., p.884).

5

De Gaulle and the Algerian Crisis 1958–1962

Michel Winock

The Algerian crisis marked de Gaulle's second rendezvous with historical destiny. His return to power in 1958 was surrounded by the same
atmosphere of high drama as his first appearance centre-stage in 1940.
He (who loved using maritime metaphors) was beyond question a man
for rough seas.

Some months prior to May 1958, the evidence of opinion polls shows
that few French people thought it likely that de Gaulle would ever return to power. For the majority, de Gaulle was a 'has been' – certainly a
respectable personality, even a glorious one, but also one who had defi-
nitely broken with national politics after the failure of the RPF. The political wilderness in which he found himself paralleled the anonymity
in which he had lived before 18 June 1940. De Gaulle was a man who
emerged from the shadows. His vocation as a providential figure was
nurtured by the manner in which he seemed to emerge into public con-
sciousness, appearing and reappearing at moments of despair in national
history.

Recalled in 1958, at a time when the Fourth Republic found itself in
an impasse over Algeria, de Gaulle had to grapple with that same
Algerian problem for four years. The stakes could not have been higher,
for they involved not only the political status of Algeria but also the very
unity of France, her internal security and her future as a great nation.
Opponents and supporters of de Gaulle took up opposing positions in
the wake of the Evian Agreements of March 1962, by which Algeria was
to gain its independence. The former denounced the general's 'betrayal',
claiming that when he returned to power in 1958 he had committed
himself to defending the cause of 'French Algeria'. The latter wanted

to demonstrate that from the beginning of the Fifth Republic de Gaulle had a clear perception of the inevitability of Algerian independence. As a great statesman and a far-seeing advocate of decolonization, he had to eliminate hostile forces in order to achieve peace, and this had inevitably involved him in using words obliquely, giving rise to possible misunderstandings.

Charles de Gaulle himself, in his *Memoirs of Hope*, wrote that on his return to power he had approached the Algerian question 'with no strictly pre-determined plan'. The situation was too complex for a clear solution to be visible. 'But', he added, 'the main lines were clear in my mind. Indeed, as early as 30 June 1955, when a large scale insurrection was taking place, I had stated at a press conference in reply to questions on the subject: "no other policy but one which aims at replacing domination by association in French North Africa is either viable or worthy of France"'.[1] Algeria, in his view, had to 'decide for itself'. Tactics, however, demanded cautious movement from one stage to the next without any proclamation of his ultimate intention.

None the less, the question remains: between 1958 and 1962 did de Gaulle simply vary his tactics, or did he change his fundamental objectives along the way? In *Vingt-huit ans de gaullisme*, Jacques Soustelle, one of the losers of French Algeria, used a series of de Gaulle's own quotations to condemn the inconsistent evolution of the President of the Republic 'from French Algeria to headlong flight'.

In June 1958, all Algerians, and the Muslims first and foremost, are 'French people with equal rights', Algeria is 'French territory today and forever'. In January 1959, Algeria is offered a 'privileged position in the (French) Community', although what that consisted of remained undefined. In September of the same year, de Gaulle announced self-determination, with three possible outcomes, condemning one of these in the severest possible terms, namely secession. In January 1960, he declared that he still favoured 'the solution which is the most French'. Two months later, he categorically eliminated this solution, recommending an 'Algerian Algeria', a brilliant formula, perhaps, but a meaningless one unless it signified purely and simply the turning over of the country to the Front de Libération Nationale (FLN). In July 1960 he let it be understood that Algeria would have its own government, in November that it would become a state, in April 1961 that this state would be independent, and in December that France was 'pulling out' and handing Algeria and its people over to the terrorists who, although beaten on the ground, were to receive from de Gaulle the gift of an unexpected political triumph.[2]

---

[1] C. de Gaulle, *Memoirs of Hope* (1970; English translation: Weidenfeld & Nicolson, London, 1971), p.44.
[2] J. Soustelle, *Vingt huit ans de gaullisme* (La Table Ronde, Paris, 1968), p.295.

Does this simply point to deliberate linguistic ambiguities by de Gaulle which were designed to disarm successive opponents? Shortly before the signature of the Evian Agreements, Louis Terrenoire, Secretary of State in the Prime Minister's Office and former Minister for Information told the Gaullist activists of the Bouches-du-Rhône that

> To speak of 'denial' is an outrage, and of change an error. De Gaulle has not altered; he is attempting to reach the goal which he has long seen as the focus of the hopes of the Muslim masses of Algeria: independence and sovereignty, but in co-operation with France.

And he went on to explain the subtleties of what Pierre Viansson-Ponté, a journalist with *Le Monde* , has called 'government by the word'.

> If General de Gaulle, concerned to prepare public opinion both politically and psychologically, has little by little clarified the expression of his thoughts, he has never wavered in these. But it is true that sometimes he has been the victim of erroneous or simplistic interpretations of his words.[3]

What is more or less established is that de Gaulle never believed in the possibility of assimilation, a solution favoured by the *pieds-noirs* and the officer corps.[4] The major difficulty arose from the fact that de Gaulle owed his return to power to the supporters of French Algeria and to French army officers who had jointly organized, or taken responsibility for, the attempted *coup* of 13 May 1958 in Algiers. This intervention by the army in French politics, without precedent since the *coup d'état* of 2 December 1851 which led to the Second Empire, might happen again, only this time against de Gaulle. He was fully aware of this, and had to combine benevolence with firmness in his handling of the officer corps down to the decisive trial of strength in April 1961, with the generals' *putsch*. The *pieds-noirs* , for their part, representing a million people or a little more than a tenth of the population of Algeria, only carried any political weight to the extent that they found protection from the army or from the alliances which their representatives concluded with nationalist politicians and pressure groups in mainland France.

In any event, de Gaulle himself never contemplated the project of assimilation so dear to the hearts of the officers. It had come too late, 'colonialism was finished'.[5] This is not to say that de Gaulle stood for

[3]*Le Monde*, 10 February 1962.
[4]That is, the European settlers in Algeria.
[5]*Memoirs of Hope*, p.56.

decolonization on principle. He was far removed from the feelings of left-wing intellectuals regarding colonialism. He refers in his writings to the 'colonial epic'. His famous Brazzaville Address of January 1944 foresaw reforms but no progress towards independence for the colonies. Cold War threats had sensitized him to the strategic importance of overseas possessions. Free France had been founded on the idea and reality of the Empire. Soustelle, from this point of view, could make hay with de Gaulle's declaration in 1951 that 'there would be no future for France if she gave up her mission in the French Union',[6] and that at the same time 'the other states and territories in the Union would be unable to find the conditions ensuring their security, liberty and progress outside'.[7] But in the meantime, events in Indochina, along with Moroccan and Tunisian independence, undoubtedly led him to believe that in the longer term (however undefined that might be) Algeria would have to govern itself.

As early as 4 June 1958 in a speech in Algiers while he was still only Prime Minister, de Gaulle announced that elections in Algeria would take place in a single electoral college, thus achieving the electoral equality which the French had always refused to the Muslim Algerians, and implying that the eventual solution of Algeria's status would be placed in their hands. 'It is with these elected representatives', de Gaulle said, 'that we shall do what has to be done'.[8] On 3 October 1958, when launching the Constantine Plan[9] which might have aroused the hopes of the supporters of a French Algeria, he declared: 'In any event, it is in the nature of things that Algeria's future will be based both on her own personality and on close solidarity with metropolitan France'.

It thus seems clear that at that moment at least, de Gaulle was not preparing public opinion for the inevitability of independence. I personally remember that declared supporters of this solution were badly shaken by the Constantine Plan which appeared to open the way for a new lease of the French presence. Yet at the same time, by insisting on the 'Algerian personality', he dissociated himself from the position of the army and the French settlers. For him, Algeria was not France.

De Gaulle's political strategy aimed at putting forward the concept of 'association'. In a first attempt, he tried to solve the Algerian question within the framework of the French Community, with whose inception in 1958 he had fundamentally reformed the French Union. This community framework, which Seko Touré's Guinea alone refused to join, was

[6]The name taken by the French Empire under the Fourth Republic.
[7]Soustelle, *Vingt huit ans de gaullisme* , p.292.
[8]*L' Année politique 1958* (Presses Universitaires de France, Paris, 1959)
[9]This plan put in train a series of measures intended to improve the situation of Muslims. Thus, an undertaking was given that one-tenth of the French places in the public service would be reserved for them, that universal education would be provided for the young, and that 25,000 hectares of arable land would be developed and distributed.

to provide the institutional space within which the future Algeria could find its place.[10] Here, its dominant Arab–Muslim personality would find expression, whereas the current organization into French departments was standing proof of its subject status.[11]

When de Gaulle solemnly proposed the road of self-determination to Algerians on 16 September 1959, the three alternative solutions which he set out were not equally desirable in his own eyes. By the tone of speech he used in designating it, he clearly rejected *francisation* (gallicization), the very term implying the impracticability of the integration demanded by the supporters of 'French Algeria'. He equally conveyed his rejection of 'secession' – a no less pejorative term describing the independence desired by Algerian nationalism. Disapproval of both these options reinforced the preferable solution in de Gaulle's eyes, which his speeches emphasized, that of 'association' – 'the government of Algerians by Algerians, supported by French aid and in close union with France'.

At what precise moment did he change his goal? It is probable that the failure of the French Community during the course of 1960, when the Black African states and Madagascar successively gained independence, influenced his decision to give up his initial plan. At the same time, in order to be successful, his policy of association needed to win the support of sufficient followers in Algeria itself. The rise of extremism on both sides, Algerian and French, removed any hope of this. The 'week of the barricades' in January 1960, as well as the sympathy shown to the European rioters of Algiers by the army, undoubtedly marked a decisive moment in the evolution of his strategy. 'Proof was given were any needed', wrote Raymond Aron, 'that Algiers could not overturn the Fifth Republic as it had toppled the Fourth or exercise a right of veto over the decisions of the government in Paris. Even more, since an attempted insurrection had failed and since the army, in spite of some hesitation, had in the end obeyed the government, observers were justified in considering that henceforth de Gaulle had more freedom of action than before.'[12]

In fact, an Algerian delegation, led by Ferhat Abbas, joined representatives of the French government in Melun, not far from Paris, from 20 to 29 June 1960 for discussions on the conditions for a cease-fire. The negotiations, which had given rise to much hope in public opinion, ended none the less in failure. A little over four months later, de Gaulle's address

---

[10] The leader of Guinea had recommended a no vote in the referendum proposed by de Gaulle in 1958.

[11] De Gaulle had made it clear that adherence to the Community was voluntary: 'No one is compelled to join. I state it here: independence is available to whoever wants it' (speech of 25 August 1958 at Conakry). Thus de Gaulle already envisaged Algerian self-determination, while hoping for voluntary 'association'.

[12] R. Aron, *L' Année politique 1960*, Introduction, p.vi.

of 4 November 1960 seemed to be preparing public opinion for the possibility of Algerian independence. He affirmed that 'Algeria will have its own government, institutions and laws'. Going further, he declared that 'the rebel leaders ... claim to be the government of the Algerian Republic, which will exist one day, but which does not exist yet'. This qualification only theoretically modified de Gaulle's affirmation of Algeria's vocation for sovereignty. But he still denied the FLN's claim to represent all Algerian Muslims. Here, de Gaulle kept to the position set forth in his broadcast of 29 January 1960: 'the rebel organization pretends that it will only accept a cease-fire if I have granted it the privilege of treatying with it alone beforehand on the political destiny of Algeria. This would be tantamount to making it the sole valid representative of Algerians and would establish it in advance as the government of the country. That I will not do'.[13]

At this stage, de Gaulle seems to have resigned himself to the inevitable. The Algerian War remained an obstacle to the diplomatic, military and political recovery of France. Decolonization had to reach its logical conclusion. But in order to achieve this, de Gaulle had at the same time to overcome the opposition to his policy, weak in metropolitan France but strong in Algeria where it could count on the army, and also to safeguard French interests in Algeria and the Sahara against the demands of the FLN.

To move forward, he needed the support of public opinion. It was this which led him to call the referendum of 8 January 1960 'concerning the organization of government in Algeria pending self-determination'. But another segment of public opinion manifested itself first, namely the Algerians themselves, on the occasion of a new trip by the general to Algeria from 9 December 1960. On 10 December, large numbers of Muslims paraded in the streets behind green flags. 'These Muslim crowds, streaming down the streets, shouting and singing, armed with sticks and waving makeshift flags, could well open the way for a new kind of legitimacy for North Africa', wrote Jacques Berque.[14] The following day, bloody confrontations took place between members of the two communities, leaving fifty dead, forty-five of them Muslim, in Algiers. The moment for 'fraternization' had passed. On the plane home, de Gaulle confided to his Minister for Information, Louis Terrenoire, that 'we must come to an arrangement with the FLN and, in any event, back them into a corner. I shall do exactly that after the referendum'.[15]

The referendum of 8 January 1961 allows the support enjoyed by the

[13] *L'Année politique 1960* , p.5.
[14] J. Berque, 'Propos pour une fin de guerre', *Le Monde* , 24 December 1960.
[15] L. Terrenoire, *De Gaulle et l' Algérie* (Fayard, Paris, 1964), p.215.

FLN to be evaluated. Calling for a boycott, the FLN could take satisfaction from an abstention rate of 40 per cent in Algeria. Abstentions were massive in the Muslim districts of the big cities. Yet the overall result was very favourable to de Gaulle – 69.5 per cent of the votes cast in Algeria and 76.44 per cent in metropolitan France – despite the fact that the communists and the communist-oriented trade union organization, the Confédération Générale du Travail (CGT), had campaigned for a no vote. This shows how little support there was on the mainland for the cause of French Algeria, upheld by Jacques Soustelle, François Valentin, Georges Bidault or André Morice, all of whom also called for a no vote but for reasons diametrically opposed to those put forward by the communists, who usually polled around 20 per cent of the vote in elections.

Strengthened by this show of public support, de Gaulle was now in a position to begin official negotiations with the Algerian Provisional Government (GPRA).[16] 'In relation to Algeria,' wrote *Le Figaro* , the President of the Republic 'is the man of the Nation.' The talks had some difficulty in getting off the ground following a declaration by Louis Joxe, Minister of State for Algerian Affairs, that he would meet the other nationalist organization, the Algerian Nationalist Movement (MNA), on the same basis as the FLN.[17] Moreover, the announcement that negotiations were to take place relaunched the activism of the French Algeria camp, of which the Organization of the Secret Army (OAS) now took over the leadership.[18] One of the most spectacular of its outrages was the assassination of the mayor of Evian.

With the failure of the first Evian talks and the upsurge in violence, de Gaulle decided to go one step further. On 11 April, during an official trip to the south-west , he declared that 'in the world today, France has nothing to gain from maintaining her sovereignty over an Algeria which wishes to choose its own destiny ... . This state will be what the Algerians want it to be. For my part, I am convinced that it will be a sovereign state internally and externally. And France will not stand in the way'.

This time, the ultimate aim of de Gaulle's policy was stripped of all ambiguity. It sought to bring about Algerian independence through the process of self-determination. At the same time, it preserved the hope of close collaboration between France and the future sovereign Algeria.

[16] The GPRA was established by the National Council of the Revolution on 19 September 1959, the FLN having designated Ferhat Abbas as its leader.

[17] The MNA of Messali Hadj was in conflict with the FLN in metropolitan France and in Algeria. The bloody settling of accounts between the two organizations had given the advantage to the FLN.

[18] The OAS, constituted by the extremists of French Algeria in February 1961, conducted counter-terrorist operations both against Algerian terrorism and against the French supporters of Algerian independence.

What obstacles lay in the path of its realization? First of all, there was the intransigence of the FLN, which refused to consider disarming before the decisive referendum, demanded the incorporation of the Sahara within the boundaries of the future Algerian state, and claimed to be the sole representatives of the Algerian people. De Gaulle also had to confront the opponents of independence, notably the OAS, which had just issued a threatening manifesto, as well as a large section of the officer corps in Algeria, which remained steadfastly opposed to any policy of 'abandoning' the colony.

It was precisely from this quarter that de Gaulle had to deal with a *putsch*, perpetrated in Algiers on the night of 21–2 April 1961 by Generals Challe (former Commander-in-Chief in Algeria), Salan, Jouhaud and Zeller. While this military leadership sought to place the army, the administration and the entire territory of Algeria under its control, the OAS extended its activity into civil society by distributing arms and leaflets and freeing French-Algerian activists from prison. The rebellion lasted less than five days. There were several reasons for this – the virtually unanimous support of mainland public opinion (including the trade-unions and parties of the left and far-left) for de Gaulle's action in applying article 16 of the Constitution, endowing him with special powers; the refusal of conscripts in Algeria to follow the rebels; and above all de Gaulle's broadcast to the nation on radio and television, on Sunday 23 April. In this, he scornfully denounced the ringleaders of the *putsch* as 'a tetrad of superannuated generals' and went on to declare, in a manner befitting the man of character whom he had described in *The Edge of the Sword*: 'In the name of France, I order that all means, I repeat all means, be employed everywhere to block the path of these men until they are removed.' The message ended with these moving words: 'Frenchwomen, Frenchmen, help me! '

Nothing was missing from such an appeal. It contained everything – resolution, national unity, mockery of the opponent, the quest for democratic solidarity against the rebels. The head of state wore his military uniform for the occasion. He also spoke as the supreme commander of the armed forces. National service conscripts, armed with transistors, had been able to listen to this solemn reminder of where their duty lay. They were called on to obey the state, founded on national sovereignty, and not those who were abusing military authority. 'I forbid any French citizen,' declared de Gaulle, 'and first and foremost any French soldier, to carry out any of (the rebel generals') orders.' De Gaulle was at the height of his powers, at this moment, and at the height of his popularity in metropolitan France.

The defeat of the *putsch*, completed on 25 April, removed a major obstacle. De Gaulle had overcome the most serious threat from his own camp. The army henceforth had no alternative but to support his policies. Those leaders most hostile to de Gaulle had been arrested or had fled. Negotiations on the future of Algeria could now begin. Discussions between the French delegation, headed by Louis Joxe, and the delegation of the GPRA, led by Belkacem Krim,[19] were to last from 20 May to 13 June 1961. Unfortunately, discussions were then broken off owing to lack of agreement on three key issues: guarantees for the non-Muslim minorities in Algeria; the fate of the Sahara; and the need for a truce before the vote on self-determination.

A deep feeling of discouragement was perceptible in French opinion following this set-back. It would take another nine months for the discussions to reach their conclusion. This last phase of the war, made worse by the outrages perpetrated by the OAS, often provoked sheer incomprehension on the part of observers. In the October 1961 issue of *Preuves*, Raymond Aron, one of the spokesmen for liberal opinion, published an article with the title 'Farewell to Gaullism'. It was a diatribe against the general's inability to make peace in Algeria, when all the conditions for this seemed to have been met. Aron was later to say that it was 'probably (the article) I most regret writing ... . It was written in a mood of ill-humour'.[20] But for precisely this reason, it conveys eloquently the sense of exasperation of a current of public opinion which was at a loss to understand what was happening. Another example of this perplexity is Gilles Martinet, writing in *France-Observateur*, on 24 August 1961, that 'the truth is that General de Gaulle no longer knows where he is going ... Wanting to decide everything, he has wound up no longer deciding anything very much. Events are determining his policies'. The absurd and tragic nature of the situation was further illustrated by the dreadful repression of a peaceful demonstration by Algerian workers in Paris, on 17 October 1961,[21] and also by the repression of an anti-OAS demonstration in the capital on 8 February 1962, when eight demonstrators were crushed to death or suffocated at the entrance of the Charonne metro station. How could the government fighting against the OAS break up demonstrations which aimed to support it in this civil war?

The negotiations which resumed and which resulted this time in the so-called Evian accords of 19 March 1962 cast a shadow over the preceding nine months, since de Gaulle had by and large accepted the FLN's conditions, especially concerning the Sahara, seen now as an integral part of Algerian territory. The dramatic upshot of these events, totally unanticipated by the accords, is well-known; the scorched-earth policies of

[19] One of the founders of the FLN, responsible for the Kabylie region, and at that time Vice-President of the GPRA.
[20] R. Aron, *Mémoires* (Julliard, Paris, 1983), p.384.
[21] See especially J.-L. Einaudi, *La Bataille de Paris* (Le Seuil, Paris, 1991)

the OAS and the hasty, massive exodus of the French settlers. This was a conclusion of apocalyptic dimensions, tarnishing the peacemaking of de Gaulle, despite its ratification by universal suffrage.[22]

Having outlined the broad sequence of events, it is time to turn to some remarks on their wider implications, emphasizing especially the significance of the Algerian War for the political destiny of de Gaulle, and hence for France. When de Gaulle returned to power in 1958, his main concern was not Algeria but rather what he called the restoration of the state. This in turn was a precondition for the resolution of all the problems confronting the French, including the Algerian question. But it so happened that this precondition was itself conditioned by the Algerian crisis. This was the impasse in which the Fourth Republic found itself regarding Algeria, and it was the events of 13 May 1958 which in fact allowed de Gaulle to return to power. From then on, the two issues were inextricably linked, and remained so for four years.

There are four connections between the political and constitutional rehabilitation of France and the Algerian drama which are worth underlining. Firstly, it was the Algerian War which gave de Gaulle the chance to found the Fifth Republic. This is a positive, or perhaps a dialectical, way of looking at the relationship. Good (if one understands by that the stabilization of the political institutions of the Republic) came out of evil (war). Without the Algerian War, de Gaulle's 'crossing of the desert' might have proved interminable. One precedent, but a failed one, for this connection between the war and political renewal is that of Paul Déroulède's attempt at constitutional revision between 1886 and 1914. He also wanted to put an end to the 'impotence' of the parliamentary regime (the 'party regime' as de Gaulle called it) and to create a plebiscitary republic which would restore to an executive based on universal suffrage the substantive power which it had lost since the crisis of 16 May 1877. But since Déroulède could not rely on legal reform (one can hardly imagine parliamentarians abolishing a parliamentary system), he tried to achieve this by a *coup*, the result of an 'alliance' between the 'people' and the army. The attempt, which took place in February 1899, was a fiasco and Déroulède was sentenced by the High Court of Justice to ten years in exile. De Gaulle was forced to withdraw from politics after the defeat of the RPF since he did not favour a non-legal solution. It was the Algerian War which provided the unhoped-for conditions for a return to power, along the lines of Déroulède's formula transposed onto Algeria, with the alliance of the street (if not of the 'people') and the army. De Gaulle did not provoke the opportune riot of 13 May 1958, but he

<hr>

[22] On 8 April 1962, 90.7 per cent of the votes cast in a referendum in metropolitan France approved the Evian accords, while on 1 July 1962, 99.7 per cent of Algerians who voted replied 'yes' to the question: 'Do you wish Algeria to become an independent state, cooperating with France under the conditions defined by the declaration of 19 March 1962?'

did nothing to prevent it. And his lieutenants, among the boldest of whom was Jacques Soustelle, were able to channel these events to de Gaulle's advantage. The last president of the Fourth Republic, René Coty, with the help of Parliament, did the rest and gave the general the assurance of legality to effect the change to a new republic.

The second connection lies in the continuation of the Algerian drama. De Gaulle knew that Algeria, having allowed him to return to power and to give France at last the constitution he wanted, might hinder his work and obstruct his project of political renovation. In this way, Algeria became a precondition in its turn. The fate of the new institutions, the restoration of France, the policy of national greatness to which he aspired, all depended on the solution which de Gaulle would be able to find to the Algerian War.

The third connection is an obvious one: it is that of the means at de Gaulle's disposal. De Gaulle, in his efforts to find a solution, could call on political and constitutional powers which were simply not available to the men of the Fourth Republic. In other words, resolving the Algerian War was the first test for the newly created political institutions. In fact, the enhanced power of the executive – no longer diluted but now personalized – gained greater approval from public opinion than from the professional politicians. The use of the referendum, the lynch-pin of Gaullian politics, turned out to be remarkably effective. No one could deny after the referendum of 8 January 1961 that de Gaulle's Algerian policy had found widespread support among the French people. The double referendum of 1962, in France and then Algeria, sealed the end of hostilities democratically. In the same way, article 16 of the new constitution, under which the head of state receives exceptional powers in times of crisis, had been tested and had proved its utility. In the face of military insubordination, it had given the President enhanced power but defined and limited by law.[23] In other words, the Algerian War and its various developments had provided some measure of justification for precisely the articles which had appeared most objectionable to those who opposed the constitution of the Fifth Republic in the name of the republican tradition, with its innate hostility to the Bonapartist model.

The final connection between the war and the political renewal of France dates from 1962. Once again, it was the Algerian War and its aftermath which inspired, or at least permitted, the completion of the

[23] Article 16 of the constitution states that 'When the institutions of the Republic, the independence of the nation, the integrity of its territory, or the carrying out of its international obligations are threatened and the regular operation of constitutional government is interrupted, the President of the Republic shall take whatever measures are required by the circumstances, after formal consultation with the Prime Minister, the Presidents of the parliamentary assemblies, and the President of the Constitutional Council. He shall inform the nation of these measures'.

constitution by the law of 6 November 1962, instituting the election of the President of the Republic by universal suffrage. De Gaulle may have hoped to introduce this final touch to the new political institutions at an earlier date, but it was the circumstances of 1962 which enabled him to confront the majority of the political parties and have it ratified by referendum. The attempt on his life by the OAS at Petit-Clamart[24] (often presented as the decisive factor), but also, and perhaps more profoundly, the prestige that he had acquired with the ending of the Algerian War, enabled him to take this step. The conclusion of the Algerian tragedy thus allowed de Gaulle to clinch the constitution of the Fifth Republic.

The influence of the Algerian War does not stop there. It is worth noting that the Algerian conflict lay behind the decolonization of Madagascar and French Black Africa, which was achieved rapidly (the French Community not having survived 1960), without armed conflict and by the democratic process. Thus the first four years of the Gaullian regime emerge as crucially important for the historian, marking a double turning point in French history – the ending of the cycle of colonialism and the installation of a republican regime which at last provided workable government.

It might reasonably be held that Algeria would sooner or later have achieved its independence, and that sooner or later France would have ceased to be a colonial power. But it was by no means inevitable that this necessary process of decolonization should have engendered the political and constitutional renewal of France itself. Here, due weight must be attributed to the role of the 'great man'. De Gaulle recognized what Machiavelli called necessity. He understood that colonial emancipation was part of the deep movement of history. His genius was to recognize this necessity, to embrace it, and to guide it towards a positive end. The end of the 'colonial adventure' challenged France to find a new kind of greatness. De Gaulle was able to turn what others – the occupants of the Fourth Republic – considered a defeat into the legitimization of a new regime. One lasting consequence, at least, of this ambition (or illusion) has been the reconciliation of the French with their political institutions – no mean achievement, given that it had eluded previous regimes since 1789.

[24] On 22 August 1962, de Gaulle's car was caught in an ambush on the road from the aerodrome at Villacoublay from whence he was returning to Colombey. The President, his wife, his son-in-law, and his chauffeur were extraordinarily lucky to survive the attack, and this added to the myth of the general's invulnerability.

6

De Gaulle and France's Role in the World

Douglas Johnson

The centenary of the birth of de Gaulle in 1990 was naturally a celebration in which historians examined his great achievements: the creation of Free France; the post-war recognition of France as a great power and as one of the occupying forces in Germany; the return to power in 1958 and the establishment of the Fifth Republic; the ending of the war in Algeria and the successful programme of decolonization; the creation of institutions that have given France political stability and permitted a programme of successful modernization. But when historians discuss his world policy they move into a different category of judgement. Here, de Gaulle is often presented as someone who was antiquated, living in the world of the past. If it was remarkable that someone who was born at the time when Bismarck and William II had a particular vision of European power politics and expansion overseas could adapt himself to more modern conceptions of warfare, it was natural that he should be unable to rid himself of the national prejudices of the period. The man who understood about tanks and nuclear warfare did not, it is said, understand that the principles of national independence had to give way to considerations of inter-dependence and European unification.

More wickedly, it is often suggested that de Gaulle often acted out of prejudice and pique. Not understanding anything about the USA (and he was known to speak about 'the so-called United States' (*les Etats-soi-disant unis*), he remembered the hostility which Roosevelt, Cordell Hull and others showed towards France in general and to him in particular; nor was he likely to forget Admiral Leahy's support for Vichy, or his suspicions that the Americans would, in 1944, wished to have installed a military government in liberated France, probably by agreement with the Vichy authorities. Whilst he always retained his admiration for Winston Churchill as a war leader, and whilst his repeated expressions for the British people were undoubtedly sincere, he probably remained influenced by an historical conviction that Great Britain was the hereditary enemy of France. With a vision that stretched over the centuries, de Gaulle saw Franco-German enmity as a development that was relatively recent and, as one who knew his Michelet, believed that it was the ambitions of English kings that had created the French sense of nation. Nor did de Gaulle ever forget the occasions when Churchill was hostile to him, either because he thought that *la France Libre* should simply play the role of a foreign legion assisting the British forces, or because Churchill was subservient to the power and influence of the United States. When de Gaulle and Churchill quarrelled on the eve of the allied invasion of France in 1944, it may not have been totally accurate that Churchill asserted that whenever he had to choose between the ocean *(le grand large)* – that is to say the United States – and France, then he would always choose the ocean. But de Gaulle believed it, or chose to believe it.[1] According to this interpretation of his policies, either he took his revenge on the British by refusing to admit them to the European Community, or he expressed the view that Great Britain, because of its much vaunted 'special relationship' with the United States, was different from the other countries of the Community.

Another interpretation of de Gaulle's world policy would give priority to domestic preoccupations. On great occasions or on small, the French population received the impression that it was de Gaulle who was the dominant figure, and consequently his prestige as a national leader was increased. Thus, the televised speech in which the British application to join the European Community was rejected, suggested that de Gaulle controlled the Community. The speeches at Phnom Penh and at Montreal (*'Vive le Québec libre'*) showed a de Gaulle who acted in the

---

[1] It is difficult to believe that Churchill actually used the words quoted by de Gaulle in the second volume of his *Mémoires de Guerre. L'Unité* (Plon, Paris, 1956) pp.223–4. De Gaulle makes Churchill say, during their meeting on 4 June 1944, on the eve of D-Day: 'Car, sachez-le! chaque fois qu'il nous faudra choisir entre l'Europe et le grand large, nous serons toujours pour le grand large'. But Churchill must have been speaking English because Ernest Bevin, one of the two British ministers present (the other being Anthony Eden), is supposed to have commented adversely on this remark, and he certainly did not understand French. The published recollections of those who were present, apart from de Gaulle (Churchill, Eden, Duff Cooper, Lord Ismay and General Béthouart) contain no reference to the phrase, nor is it to be found in the Cabinet papers. It is, of course, true that the meeting was a stormy one and that de Gaulle and Churchill had some violent disagreements. It was perhaps unfortunate that General Smuts was present, since, in a widely publicized speech he had expressed the view that France would never be a great power again. But the words are probably de Gaulle's interpretation of what Churchill meant, rather than an accurate record.

tradition of French greatness throughout the world and who was prepared to speak firmly, even aggressively, to '*les Anglo-Saxons*' in the name of France. In innumerable small towns, as he toured France, de Gaulle would speak of the role of France in the world, and would thus avoid the more humble tasks of a head of government, obliged to consider the price of artichokes, the statistics of unemployment or the state of the motor-car industry. In Gaullist philosophy, if France was not great and did not possess a sense of destiny, then France would be devoured by the interior demons that inherited her. As a skilful politician de Gaulle also understood the advantages that could be gained from an apparent supremacy in world affairs.[2]

Others have been even less appreciative of de Gaulle's interventions in world affairs. They accused him of being out of touch with reality, living in a world of the past, when France was a great power, vitally important in European and extra-European diplomacy, powerful in military terms, influential as the leader of civilization. This had long ceased to be the case, and most obviously so after 1940. Thus de Gaulle's pronouncements, however eloquent, were empty and meaningless. He had to be compared to a Walter Mitty, living in a world of pure imagination. At times, it was as if his eloquence and lack of any sense of proportion had got the better of him. This was most obvious in his *Vive le Québec libre* speech in Montreal (24 July 1967) where, according to one interpretation, he was so exalted by his tumultuous reception that he pronounced words which, on reflection, he would never have spoken (and there is some evidence for this, since he is reported as saying that after an

[2] The importance that de Gaulle attached to foreign policy and to France's role in the world is reflected in the number of studies which have been devoted to this aspect of his activity. Spreading over the years, one can refer to the following: A. Grosser, *La politique extérieure de la Cinquième République* (Editions du Seuil, Paris, 1965); W. W. Kulski, *De Gaulle and the World* (Syracuse University Press, 1966); G. de Carmoy, *The Foreign Policies of France, 1944–1968* (University of Chicago Press, London, 1970) ; S. Serfaty, *De Gaulle and Europe* (Johns Hopkins Press, Baltimore, 1968); C.L. Sulzberger, *The Last of the Giants* (Macmillan, New York, 1970); E. L. Mosse, *Foreign Policy and Independence in Gaullist France* (Princeton University Press, 1973); E. A. Kolodziey, *French International Policy under de Gaulle and Pompidou: the Politics of Grandeur* (Cornell University Press, 1974). All biographies of de Gaulle have naturally devoted much space to his vision of France in the world. The most recent and considerable surveys are to be found in the publications which marked the centenary of his birth, and whilst questions of foreign policy are to be found in all the volumes, one should consult the following in particular: Institut Charles de Gaulle, *De Gaulle et son siècle , tome IV: La sécurité et l'indépendance de la France* (La Documentation Française-Plon, Paris, 1992); Ibid., *tome 5: l'Europe* (La Documentation Française-Plon, Paris, 1992); Ibid. *tome VI: Liberté et dignité des peuples* (La Documentation Française-Plon, Paris, 1992). Questions of foreign policy occur frequently in the seminars organized by the History Department of University College London, and the Institut Charles de Gaulle, Paris, published in *Espoir*, no.43, (June, 1983).

extraordinary reception from the French–Canadian people, *'il fallait bien que je leur dise quelquechose'*).[3]

Thus many assessments of de Gaulle's world vision have been critically hostile or dismissive. Also, perhaps inevitably, one finds there the same uncertainty concerning his fundamental policies. Just as, during the period of Free France, the British Foreign Office was reliably informed that de Gaulle had Fascist associations, and then, from sources which claimed to be equally reliable, that he had left-wing tendencies; just as the leader of the provisional government in Algiers and in Paris brought the communists into his administrations and then, as leader of the RPF, became the principal denunciator of the communists (*'les séparatistes'*) and their Soviet masters; so one naturally assumes that de Gaulle had no lasting or fixed principles. There was no such thing as 'Gaullism', there was only 'de Gaullism'. Like other politicians de Gaulle adapted his policies to circumstances, and whatever were the eloquent rationalizations that followed the event, they did not represent a policy that was either constant or fixed. Furthermore, if one considers de Gaulle as one who simply followed *la politique politicienne* (political expediency) whilst denouncing it, then one has to note his frequent lack of success.[4]

It is clear that one needs to examine certain fundamental issues in de Gaulle's policy. The first, and the most obvious concerns his attitude towards France's colonies. It was not only those who, in 1958, believed that de Gaulle was a supporter of *l'Algérie française* who were surprised when he became the champion of an independent Algeria. There are also those who have found a contrast between the de Gaulle who was the champion of the French Empire in the 1940s and 1950s, and who became the architect of decolonization in subsequent years (although, it is worth noting, he never liked to use the word 'decolonization'). There is plenty of evidence to show that de Gaulle was a believer in France's colonial empire. Well before the war, in 1934, he wrote that 'the many bonds that

[3] The criticisms of de Gaulle's world policy, whether made by British or French observers, usually concentrated on the disproportion that existed between his apparent ambitions and the means that were at his disposal. See, for example, M. Duverger, *Le Monde*, 22–3 March 1964, and Denis Healey, *The Times*, 1 June 1965. For general criticisms of de Gaulle's policies, see D. Pickles, *The Uneasy Entente*, (Chatham House Essays, Oxford, 1966); J. Newhouse, *De Gaulle and the Anglo-Saxons*, (Deutsch, London, 1970). Concerning the 'Vive le Québec libre' speech, it is true that de Gaulle spoke of it as a personal gesture – 'Je n'aurais pas été de Gaulle si je ne l'avais pas fait' (P.-L. Mallen, *Vivre le Québec libre* [Plon, Paris, 1978], p.155) – but he had been insistently solicited to make the journey ('Mon Général, le Québec a besoin de vous'). See A. and P. Rouanet, *Les trois derniers chagrins de Général de Gaulle* (Grasset, Paris, 1980) and J. Ethier-Blais, 'A quel Québec de Gaulle s'adressait-il?', *Espoir*, September 1992, pp.61–6. See also *De Gaulle et son siècle*, tome.VI, pp.509–606.

[4] These questions are discussed in many of the contributions to *Approches de la philosophie politique du Général de Gaulle* (Institut Charles de Gaulle, Paris, 1983)

link metropolitan France with its overseas possessions are growing all the time'. But even he had not shared the common myth of French greatness being assured by the extension of French power into non-European territories, until he came to London in 1940 and became necessarily a supporter of colonial France. It was when the colonies in Africa and in Oceania proclaimed their support for Free France that his position changed.[5] The Foreign Office did not fail to notice that whereas by an exchange of personal letters between de Gaulle and Churchill, the former had been recognized merely as the leader of those who called themselves Free French, the rallying of French colonies meant that the Free French leader had become an administrator of territories.[6] The colonies not only provided him with a reservoir of men, but also gave him the strategic space he required to escape from the stranglehold of London.[7] Although he never carried out his threat to establish his headquarters in Brazzaville, he was determined to profit from the fact that *'l'homme de Londres'* was also *'l'homme de Brazzaville.'* Therefore it could be said that de Gaulle had not become the leader of Free France in order to preside over the dissolution of the French Empire, 'the territories linked to our destiny, that have remained loyal'.

However, it was also necessary to appeal to the populations of these territories, and de Gaulle found it all the easier to do this because he recognized that, with the war, certain changes were inevitably taking place in the colonies. Speaking in London, 23 October 1941, he said 'Yes indeed, this war, which has in many ways been a revolution, could lead to a profound and worthwhile transformation of Africa, despite the blood and the tears that are flowing, and will continue to flow'. And at Constantine, 12 December 1943, he spoke of the aid which North Africa was giving to France and of the obligations which this created and which would have to be met, at some time in the future. These considerations led to the Brazzaville conference, which was held in January–February 1944. It promised to give colonial peoples representation in the conduct of their affairs, and it was preoccupied with the need to improve the

[5] These questions are discussed in J. Lacouture, *De Gaulle. The Rebel, 1890–1944* (Harvill-Collins, London, 1990), chapter 22.
[6] A special meeting to consider these questions was held at the Foreign Office on 6 September 1940. It was noted that de Gaulle was sometimes calling himself 'chef de la France libre', that is to say, the ruler of a territory: *Public Record Office*, FO 371 24340.
[7] One example, among many, of de Gaulle's calculations on this issue, can be found in 1942. 'The second factor which worried London was obviously my presence in a territory of the French Empire at a time when the English preferred to retain control over my movements and my public statements.' – De Gaulle to René Pleven and Maurice Dejean, 10 September 1942, in *Lettres, Notes et Carnets: juillet 1941–mai 1943* (Plon, Paris, 1982), pp.380–1. This is all the more significant because de Gaulle was able to foresee the Allied landings in North Africa two months later, an operation which was secret and of which he had not been informed.

standard of living in these countries. However, it did not envisage the eventuality of self-government, and it stated with deliberate firmness that any idea of autonomy, or of the possibility of evolution outside the French organization of these territories, had to be set aside. Thus de Gaulle's reforms were limited.[8]

Nothing illustrates better his approach to these problems than the question of Indo-China which was in the anomalous position of being governed by Vichy and indirectly governed by the Japanese, until March 1945 when the Japanese took over full control. De Gaulle prepared an expeditionary force of two divisions to be sent to the Far East but by the time it arrived, in the autumn of 1945, Japan had capitulated (2 September 1945). British and Chinese troops had intervened and Ho Chi Minh had assumed power in the name of the Front of National Independence. But de Gaulle retained his view that France was responsible for Indo-China and should exercise its sovereign rights in that territory. He resisted negotiating with the idea of independence in mind and even after his resignation in January 1946 he seems to have persisted in this view. There is some uncertainty as to why he advised General Leclerc not to return to Indo-China as supreme commander in 1946. The simplest interpretation is that he believed that Leclerc would not receive adequate support from the weak governments which were then succeeding each other. But it is also possible that he distrusted Leclerc's leaning towards granting autonomy to the different states of the Indo-Chinese Union (as had been foreshadowed in the policies of Saintény). In a speech at Bordeaux, 15 May 1947, he spoke to the need for each territory to develop its own personality, but within a 'a kind of association' with France. And this meant that the authority of France should be exercised 'on the spot', and should be present in the domains of public order, national defence, foreign policy and in those economic matters that were common both to the mother country and to the dependency.[9]

Thus it can be seen that de Gaulle's vision of an evolution towards decolonization was very limited. One can cite examples of a different attitude. On 25 October 1944, commenting on the Brazzaville proceedings, he defined French policy as that of leading its peoples to the point where each would administer, and later govern itself. In 1945, receiving news of events in Indo-China, he remarked brusquely to his future son-in-law, de Boissieu, 'Well, that will all end in independence'.[10] But isolated

---

[8] *De Gaulle et son siècle, tome VI*, pp.11–85. For de Gaulle's speech at Brazzaville, 30 January 1944, see *Discours et Messages*, Vol.1 (Plon, Paris, 1970), p.373.

[9] *De Gaulle et son siècle, tome VI*, pp.456–76. See also Thierry d'Argenlieu, *Chroniques d'Indo-Chine* (Albin Michel, Paris, 1985); *Le Général Leclerc et l'Indochine* (Publications de l'Association Leclerc, Paris, 1992); *De Gaulle et le Tiers Monde* (Paris and Nice, 1980).

[10] General de Boissieu's recollection of this remark was made at the colloquium on 'Leclerc et l'Indochine', held in October 1990.

phrases, and the occasional epigram are not the equivalent of his decision to use force in Indo-China, as in Damascus, or his decision to quell the Algerian rising in Sétif (May 1945).[11] De Gaulle's enemies would say that both the war in Indo-China and the war in Algeria stemmed from these policies and they are not alone in being cynical about the fact that it was de Gaulle who brought the Algerian War to an end. However, there are sound reasons for de Gaulle's policies in the 1940s, and for their subsequent evolution. During the war he realized how American policy sought to exclude France from exercising any sovereignty over its territories in North Africa or Madagascar (except under a humiliating tutelage) and envisaged putting Indo-China under international trusteeship. Thus his 'colonialism' was a defence of France against America (which brought him, at times, into a closer relationship with Churchill). After the conclusion of hostilities de Gaulle was convinced of the possibility of a new war breaking out. In August 1945, when he met President Truman, the two agreed, in de Gaulle's words, that 'the rivalry between the free world and the Soviet bloc would dominate everything from now on'. In those circumstances, and with the Red Army 'two stages of the Tour de France' from Paris, it was essential that France should retain its possessions in the West Indies, in Africa, in the Indian Ocean and the Far East. Still less should France give power to a communist leader such as Ho Chi Minh. But perhaps what was most important for de Gaulle, was that if France were to proceed to some decolonization, then it should be seen to be a French initiative, the action of a strong and independent state. It could not be a concession to international or nationalist pressure.

It was natural that de Gaulle's ideas evolved as the situation evolved. No one any longer took seriously American hostility to French colonialism (even when made by a certain Senator John F. Kennedy). The death of Stalin in 1953 lessened the dangers of war. The war in Indo-China turned out to be disastrous and the French abandoned their positions in that country, as in Tunisia and Morocco. Although de Gaulle could not approve of these humiliations, which were for him symptoms of the essential weakness of the Fourth Republic, he was never a man who sought to put the clock back or who would wilfully neglect realities. The ending of the RPF (it was two years later, in his press conference of June 1955, that he said 'I am taking my leave of you, and it will doubtless be for a long time'; but interestingly enough he also referred, on the same occasion, to the Sultan of Morocco) gave him greater freedom. He undertook long journeys in different parts of Africa. He was well informed about the difficulties of the war in Algeria. He knew that more and more

---

[11] For de Gaulle and Algeria, see *De Gaulle et son siècle, tome VI*, pp.86–184. See also de Gaulle's speech at Algiers of 12 October 1947: 'France's authority must therefore be affirmed as clearly and as strongly as on any other territory belonging to her.' *Discours et Messages* (Plon, Paris, 1970), p.132.

politicians, officials and commentators were turning to him as someone who could resolve the everlasting problems of France's colonial empire. Many historians have distorted the question by arguing as to whether or not de Gaulle had decided, before he came to power in 1958, in favour of Algerian independence. Whatever his innermost convictions, he was prepared to adapt his policy to the circumstances that prevailed. But certain principles were constant. The first was that a Gaullist constitution should be installed in France. The second was that France should take the initiative and be the dominant partner in all negotiations with the representatives of the overseas territories whoever they were. The third was that France should not get caught up in endless colonial conflicts that would weaken, if not paralyse, French action in Europe and in the world at a time when crucial changes were taking place.

It was shown that France had the initiative when de Gaulle toured Africa in September 1958, presenting the new constitution which provided for a Franco-African community. 'If you want independence, this is your chance' was his message. Only Guinea chose this manner of breaking with France, but the Franco-African community did not last and de Gaulle saw to it that it disappeared 'without upheavals' whilst preserving important linkages with France. The essential reasons for its failure were the divisions that existed amongst the African leaders themselves, and whilst de Gaulle had undoubtedly nourished ideas of 'a new association', he seems to have readily abandoned them. It could be that he had a hope of Algeria joining in some association with France, and there were speeches in which he envisaged a French programme for economic development, or a partition of the country in which France would retain the rich resources of the Saharan territories. But the process whereby France moved from 'French Algeria' (a phrase that was used only once by de Gaulle, at Mostaganem, in June 1958), to 'self-determination' and then to independence, was regulated by de Gaulle, by his speeches, by the strict instructions that he gave his negotiators (both those who were secret and those who were official) and by the referenda that he organized in France. Hence the Evian agreements of 1962, which ended the war in Algeria, appeared more as a triumph than a humiliation for France. De Gaulle had dominated the timing of events. He had retained a linkage between all former French territories and France, something he considered to be essential. And this permitted the preservation of another essential element in France's relations with the rest of the world, '*la Francophonie*'. That is to say, the acceptance of the cultural mission of France and a certain unity of all who spoke French.[12]

De Gaulle responded ruthlessly to the Algerian question. He had not been interested in the army's plans for further offensives and he

[12]See 'Quelques aspects de l'influence culturelle de la France', *Espoir*, 86, September 1992.

abandoned with a certain ease those who had been counting upon France, whether as settlers or as Algerian volunteers for the French Army (the *harkis*). But he realized that he might have to take some action with regard to the French Army which had become a centre of dissatisfaction and which risked becoming even more dangerous to legitimate authority unless it was reorganized. The need to streamline the French defence structure, to entrust it to a new leadership and to give it a new mission coincided remarkably with de Gaulle's policies in a number of other areas. De Gaulle always believed in the necessity for France to be independent and for this it was necessary for France to have an effective defence force. Times without number he explained what was for him the fundamental fact of French history, that the necessities of defence were always at the origins of the state. If a regime could not withstand invasion, or attack, then it collapsed. The justification of every government was therefore its ability to defend France. In the twentieth century this meant that an independent foreign policy had to be sustained by an independent defence policy. 'The defence of France must be French', as he put it. And this defence had to be nuclear. The Provisional Government led by de Gaulle created the Commissariat à l'Energie Atomique (Atomic Energy Commission) in October 1945; many of his associates and supporters helped to guide the atomic energy programme towards nuclear armament in the days of the Fourth Republic; once back in power, it was he again who decided that the first test explosion of the French atomic bomb should take place in the early months of 1960.[13]

Naturally, all those who oppose nuclear weapons have regretted this. But de Gaulle has been criticized more particularly for three reasons. Firstly, because it was said that France was too small and too weak a power to carry out such a programme and to succeed in creating an effective weapon. At best, it was said, France would have *'une bombette'*. Secondly, because France was protected, as was Western Europe in general, by American nuclear power. The corollary of de Gaulle's nuclear policy, which was to leave the North Atlantic Treaty Organization, was an example of foolish and personal anti-Americanism, which had no justification in policy. Thirdly, there was no power which was threatening France in particular. If there was a possibility of a Soviet move against the West, then France was but one of a whole series of powers which would be affected. There was no need for France to have an independent nuclear deterrent. To insist on having one was simply an expensive attempt to gain some sort of meaningless prestige, meaningless in the sense that relations between France and other states would not be affected by their knowledge of the existence of a nuclear arsenal that was probably destined to remain unused.

[13] *De Gaulle et son siècle, tome IV*, pp.11–217.

The answers to these criticisms were simple enough, but they have only become absolutely clear with the passage of time. Firstly, France was able to sustain its policies financially, and they have all been adopted by de Gaulle's successors, without exception. By 1969, the year of de Gaulle's resignation, the Mirage IV bombers were fully operational, the Intermediate Range Ballistic Missiles were almost ready, and de Gaulle had launched the first missile carrying tactical nuclear warheads. Financial difficulties were, and are, always predicted. Technological weaknesses have always existed. But the programme has been accomplished and far from being derisory, it is impressive.

Secondly, shortly before coming to power, de Gaulle had seen confirmation in the Suez affair of 1956 that American interests and policies in no way coincided with those of France. If France abandoned its defence to the United States then it was at the mercy of the United States deciding, for its own reasons of world policy, to fight a limited nuclear war. France was also at the mercy of the United States coming to an agreement with the Soviet Union and withdrawing from Europe. De Gaulle understood the complexities of the Soviet–American relationship, with its mixtures of collaboration and competition. It was not the result of some personal anti-Americanism that caused France to withdraw from the structures of the North Atlantic Treaty Organisation in 1966. It was an attempt to normalize Franco-American relations, and it permitted de Gaulle to remain a member of that Atlantic alliance, and to support the United States at moments of tension, such as the Cuban missile crisis.

Thirdly, it was inconceivable that a great power should decide that it had no enemies and that it did not need to be preoccupied with the defence of its territories. De Gaulle explained what he had said to Kennedy in June 1961. 'I can only confirm to him France's intention of becoming a nuclear power. For her, it is the the only way of ensuring that no one can risk killing her without risking his own death.'[14] The very fact that there was a stalemate between the superpowers reinforced the autonomy of the lesser powers. A state possessing nuclear weapons could not be ignored in any settlement where that state had interests. When Franco-German relations were reviewed, the fact that France was a nuclear power and in a position to defend West Germany, meant that France was always the dominant partner (in de Gaulle's time).

Once one has mentioned Germany, then one has to approach the whole problem of the role of Europe in de Gaulle's concept of world affairs,. Once again, he has been criticized for being old-fashioned and more particularly for being nationalistic, that is to say, putting French

[14]De Gaulle's account of his meeting with Kennedy is in *Memoirs of Hope* pp.267–8. See F. Costigliola, 'Kennedy, de Gaulle et le défi de la consultation entre alliés', *De Gaulle et son siècle, tome IV*, pp.254–66.

interest before any conception of European unity. As Harold Macmillan once put it, when he talked of Europe he meant France. Yet although he had been reported as saying in 1957 that if he returned to power he would tear up the Treaty of Rome (and one should remember that one of the few politicians of the Fourth Republic whom he admired, Pierre Mendès France, voted against the Treaty when it was debated in 1957), he decided to honour the signature of his predecessors. He thus accepted the European Community and Euratom, and the existence of these agreements made it all the more necessary, in his eyes, for France to recover its financial and monetary position and to establish a stable and strong government.

It is comparatively easy to show that de Gaulle had always been European in the sense that he had always thought in terms of some sort of association amongst Europeans, whether it was 'an association amongst Slavs, Germans, Gauls and Latins', or an association which included European peoples 'from Iceland to Istanbul and from Gibraltar to the Urals'. In his memoirs he described his policy from 1940 onwards as being one of persuading the states along the Rhine, the Alps and the Pyrenees to form a political, economic and strategic bloc, which would become one of the three planetary powers and which could therefore, should it become necessary, act as the arbiter between the Soviet and the American camps. It was said by many that this statement was a rationalization of certain attitudes and statements that were made in the unusual situation that de Gaulle found himself in, and that it should not be taken over-seriously. Nevertheless there is reason to believe that these ideas represent a constant preoccupation. He saw two important factors regarding Western Europe. The fact that none of the geographical issues which had been at the centre of disputes in the past, the Rhine, the Alps, the Low Countries, the Pyrenees, the Channel, the Mediterranean, any longer set any country against any other. And the fact that all the countries of Western Europe were conscious of their relative decline in world power. But since history had given them both the talent and the habit of *grandeur*, they realized how this could be recovered by building Western Europe into a political, economic, cultural and human group, organized for action, progress and defence.

The principles were clear. Firstly, Western Europe should be economically, politically and militarily an independent union. It should never be part of an Atlantic community dominated by the United States. There were two implications for this. One was that France had to be the leader. The five partners would not have the will-power to resist American pressure, unless France led them. The other was, as de Gaulle explained to Macmillan in June 1962, that British entry would not only alter the character of the Community, both politically and economically, but it would weaken the Community's independence from the United States, since

Britain was too tied, and too contented to be tied, to the United States.

The second principle was that the European Community should be based upon the co-ordination of the policies of its member states. There should not be supra-national institutions that should overrule the 'Europe of states'. The consequences of this were that within this community of states it was essential that the two most powerful of them, France and Germany, should work together and should establish an understanding. This alliance, if it were to dominate the Community, would be all the more acceptable to France because it would itself be dominated by a France that was a united state and a nuclear power. The other consequence was that de Gaulle launched himself into a series of negotiations, heralded by the memorandum of 17 September 1958 (sent to Eisenhower and Macmillan), and dominated by his meetings with Adenauer, the Fouchet Commission that was set up in 1961, and various initiatives taken by the Quai d'Orsay in the course of 1962 and 1963. Observers have often forgotten that these negotiations were not successful, in spite of the suppleness of de Gaulle's diplomacy which was in contrast to the brutality that he employed on other occasions. It was because of these failures that de Gaulle changed his tactics: he turned to Russia in 1966, and the so-called Soames affair in 1969 suggests that he was also prepared to turn to England. But the objective concerning a *Europe des Etats* remained, whether via a Franco-Soviet agreement concerning German reunification or a pact of European security which would be supported by Britain and the United States.[15]

De Gaulle was prepared to change his ideas and his methods. But he was never a pragmatist. He would never bend conviction to comport with expediency.[16] He believed in activity and thought it vital that France should be present in every sector of world diplomacy. It was necessary for France to assume greatness and to say so. And with it all, one had to be realistic. 'One can regret the elegance of oil lamps, the splendour of sailing ships, the charm of their crews; but in the end, the only politics that matter are those that take account of realities.'[17]

[15] The story of de Gaulle's European policies has been studied very many times. It can most easily be reviewed now in *De Gaulle et son siècle* , *tome V*. For his attitude towards Britain one should consult both the memoirs of Harold Macmillan: *The Blast of War, 1939–1945* (Macmillan, London, 1967); *Tides of Fortune, 1945–1955* (Macmillan, London, 1969); *Riding the Storm, 1956–1959* (Macmillan, London, 1971); *Pointing the Way, 1959–1961* (Macmillan, London, 1972). See also A. Horne, *Macmillan*, 2 vols. (Macmillan, London, 1988 and 1989); and F. de la Serre, *La Grande-Bretagne et la communauté européenne* (Paris, 1987)

[16] It is not enough to say, as is said, that de Gaulle was not a man who negotiated, but was one who declaimed, dictated, made sweeping concessions in the grand manner and said 'no' in the grand manner (Newhouse, *De Gaulle and the Anglo-Saxons*, pp.234–5). De Gaulle was, as we are constantly learning, a most attentive, skilfull and determined negotiator.

[17] *Discours et messages, tome I*, pp.227–8.

7

De Gaulle as Politician and Christian

Jean-Marie Mayeur

Central to any attempt to understand de Gaulle's thoughts and actions is a parallel consideration of the man as a politician and as a Christian. He was often accused of being excessively arrogant, of lacking humanity, of being a disciple of Machiavelli or of Maurras. One of his former ministers, the Christian Democrat Pierre-Henri Teitgen, formulated the question thus in his memoirs: 'Did he put politics above or below morality? Was he, as many saw him, the archangel of politics, the incarnation of the Platonic myth, or was he a kind of Machiavellian genius?' Teitgen offers a cautious conclusion: 'I think he was both at the same time'.[1] The question remains an extraordinarily difficult one. André Malraux, himself an agnostic, was aware of the depth of de Gaulle's faith and noted in *Fallen Oaks* that 'his faith was not a question, it was basic, like France. But he liked to speak of his France; he did not like to speak of his religion'.[2] This observation underlines the limits and difficulties of a field of enquiry where researchers have often had to be content with fragments of evidence, or less. Yet on the basis of a number of testimonies, of various published works and memoirs, and especially of the invaluable *Lettres, notes et carnets*, edited by Philippe de Gaulle, it is possible to suggest some kind of answer to Teitgen's questions.

---

[1] P.-H. Teitgen, *Faites entrer le témoin suivant? 1940–1958, de la Résistance à la Ve République* (Ouest-France, Rennes, 1988).
[2] A. Malraux, *Fallen Oaks. Conversation with de Gaulle* (1971; English translation: Hamish Hamilton, London, 1972), p.87.

A Catholic by tradition

In order to measure the intensity of Charles de Gaulle's religious feeling, it is necessary to look back at his origins and formative years. At the beginning of his *War Memoirs*, de Gaulle wrote of his mother, a devout Christian with two sisters who became nuns of the Sacred Heart Order, that she had 'an uncompromising passion for France, equal in strength to her religious piety'. The phrase is a strong one. Piety denotes a form of Christianity founded on a personal spiritual life which finds expression in both practice and devotions. But it should not surprise us that this piety went side by side with patriotism. French Catholics of the late nineteenth century could not dissociate their allegiance to the Church from their allegiance to France.

The influence of de Gaulle's father on his upbringing was no less considerable than that of his mother. At a time when many fathers scarcely intervened in their children's education or, out of deference to the Church, remained detached from it, Henri de Gaulle followed his children's education closely. He was also a convinced Catholic. In his youth he had helped found a students' organization which came to be called the Olivaint Conference, after the execution of the Jesuit priest who was their chaplain at the time of the Commune.[3] Later in life, he lived, according to his niece Geneviève, 'not just as a practising Catholic but as a devout one'. Like his friend Jules Auffray, he simultaneously admired both Joseph de Maistre,[4] and Montalembert and Ozanam, thus reconciling counter-revolutionaries with liberal Catholicism in a symbiosis which up-ends the overly systematic classifications of the historians of ideas. An enemy of Jacobin revolutionary ideology, Henri de Gaulle, like many of the generation which came of age at the end of the Second Empire, had been influenced by the ideas propagated in the *Correspondant* which aimed at bridging the gap between the Church and modern liberalism. While he did not accept all the tenets of liberal Catholicism, he supported the idea of the lay Christian's involvement in political life which provided him with a certain sense of the freedom of the Christian within the Church, as opposed to what might be characterized as clericalism or the ultramontane tradition.[5]

Henri de Gaulle's considerable influence on his family and his students (he was a secondary school principal) makes it important to establish his

[3] See B. Auffray, *Un Homme politique sous la Troisième République, Jules Auffray, 1852–1916* (Pensée Universelle, Paris, 1972). My grateful acknowledgement to Mme Odile Rudelle who made me aware of the existence of this work.
[4] He gave a conference on de Maistre at the end of which he developed the idea that the source of authority comes from the people (Auffray, *Un Homme politique*, p.44).
[5] 'Veuillot commits the immense error of turning the Catholic religion into a political party' wrote J. Auffray (Auffray, *Un Homme politique*, p.47).

early orientation. A man of tradition, a 'nostalgic monarchist' (i.e. legiti-
mist) and a 'representative of the old, the true France' according to the
inscription on his tombstone, he none the less stood apart from his social milieu by refusing to participate in its predominant anti-Dreyfusism.
A quarter of a century later, he faithfully obeyed the Vatican's instructions and gave up reading the *Action Française* when Maurras's organization, which had never held his unquestioning allegiance, was banned.

From his family background, then, Charles de Gaulle inherited a
staunch attachment to the Catholic Church. Yet this unfailing support
was inseparable from a sense of independence from the hierarchy. This
needs to be underlined, for it more accurately identifies de Gaulle's attitude than any explanation in terms of Gallicanism – a complex term and
one which has to be used very cautiously in this case.[6]

There are relatively few indications as to the kind of education Charles
de Gaulle received in religious schools, first with the Christian Brothers
and then with the Jesuits. We do know, however, that when a pupil of
the latter he joined a religious group known as the 'Congregation of the
Holy Virgin'. We also know that at secondary school he attended a
retreat in Notre-Dame du Haut Mont in Mouvaux, and gave the formal
speech of thanks to the officiating priest on behalf of the other pupils.
The Jesuits who ran Notre-Dame du Mont had links with the Association of Catholic Employers of the *Nord*, which brought social Catholic
employers together in a paternalist spirit.[7] While at his final school, the
College of the Sacred Heart at Antoing, in Belgium, Charles de Gaulle
published a small study of the Jesuits, in which he looked at the history
of the order from the end of the sixteenth century and described the life
of the congregation founded by Father Ronsin at the time of the Empire,
paying particular attention to religious practices such as the singing of
the *Veni Creator* or the *Ave Maris Stella*.[8] He noted that the congregation
had founded the Société des Bonnes Etudes at the Restoration which,
imbued with his father's influence, he described as 'a kind of Olivaint
conference'. The fact that the young student wrote this text, probably on
request, shows the depths of his links with the Jesuits.

As an adult, Charles de Gaulle remained a practising Catholic, which
in his particular milieu was less self-evident than is usually assumed.[9]
His religious practice was not a matter of simple propriety. Recalling a stay
at her uncle's in Metz, before the war, Geneviève de Gaulle remembers him

[6] As recalled by René Brouillet.
[7] R. Talmy, *Une Forme hybride du catholicisme social en France. L'Association catholique des
patrons du Nord, 1884–1895* (Mémoires et travaux publiés par des professeurs et des
facultés catholiques, Lille, 1962).
[8] C. de Gaulle, *Articles et écrits* (Plon, Paris, 1975), pp.28–32.
[9] See the letters to his mother at the beginning of the First World War in C. de Gaulle,
Lettres, notes et carnets, ed. P. de Gaulle (Plon, Paris, 1980–1), Vol. 1, pp.81–3, 148.

taking part in the solemn High Mass and being a regular Sunday communicant. This is a significant detail, since attendance at mass was not ordinarily accompanied by communion at this period, most people reserving the latter for the major religious festivals, or Easter, in accordance with the Church's requirements.

Many testimonies confirm that de Gaulle was always regular in his religious practice. In September 1944, Father Jean Daniélou was called by Claude Mauriac to celebrate mass in the Ministry of War. In the Elysée Palace, de Gaulle had the chapel, which had long since been converted into an office, reconsecrated. His nephew, Father François de Gaulle, a White Father Missionary, came to celebrate mass there whenever he was in the capital: 'You are not the Elysée chaplain', his uncle told him.[10] When visiting the provinces, the general attended Sunday mass in the company of his wife. The prefect's absence on such occasions clearly shows the private nature of this church attendance.[11] We also know that on his trips to the USSR, de Gaulle attended mass in St Louis des Français in Moscow, on Sunday 3 December 1944, and in Notre-Dame de Lourdes on Sunday 22 June 1961.[12]

This deeply rooted faith went hand in hand, according to witnesses, with a great deal of discretion. He refused to be interviewed or to answer questions on the matter, according to Georges Boursin, writing in *La Vie Catholique* after the general's death. This discretion was due to de Gaulle's personality, to an almost classical tradition of refusing to talk about oneself, to respect for the beliefs of others, and above all to respect for the exercise of power and for the secular nature of the republican state.

It would be wrong to see such discretion as the reflection of a ritualistic religious practice determined either by social usage or by a blind and simple faith. Many signs hint at the depth of the general's faith, which was well understood by those close to him. This faith was twice put to the test – that of combat in 1914, which (as he said to Geneviève de Gaulle on returning from captivity) had 'laminated his soul', and that of the birth of a mentally retarded daughter. To Canon Bourgeon, the chaplain serving with his division in 1940 who was to say mass for his daughter on 2 June, de Gaulle said 'Believe me, chaplain, this is a terrible ordeal for a father. But for me this child is also an incarnation of grace. She is my joy. She helps me to reach beyond all the failures and all the honours, always to look higher'.[13] After the death of Anne de Gaulle, he simply said 'her soul was in a body not made for her'.[14] De Gaulle thus rose to

---

[10] Another White Father, Father de Montclos, was chaplain at the Elysée Palace.
[11] As recalled by G. Galichon, a senior official at the Elysée Palace.
[12] Father Wenger, *Rome et Moscou* (Centurion, Paris, 1987), p.616.
[13] 'En ce temps-là de Gaulle', in S. Fumet, *Histoire de Dieu dans ma vie* (Fayard-Mame, Paris, 1978).
[14] As recalled by Geneviève de Gaulle.

the spiritual experience of suffering. He also demonstrated a remarkable theological certainty. Geneviève de Gaulle recalls that when the Archbishop of Rouen once expressed his regret at having broken the host during holy communion, de Gaulle replied that Christ was present in all fragments of the host.

General de Gaulle never tried to hide his deepest convictions. The leader of the Free French declared himself to be 'a soldier and a French Catholic'.[15] As head of the Republic, he respected the distinction between personal and public spheres imposed by the principle of secularism, while still allowing himself to refer to God or to pledge his 'filial attachment' to the various Popes in Rome. The words are his own and affirm his Catholicism.

In an address, delivered in Rome on 31 May 1967, to the French ecclesiastical community, he proclaimed his faith in the Church and in France: 'The Church is eternal and France will not die. The main thing for her is that she remain faithful to what she is and consequently to all the links that exist between her and the Church'. His conclusion contained a deeply felt personal hope: 'Whatever the dangers, the crises and the tragedies that we have to confront, above all and always, we know where we are heading. We are heading towards life, even as we die'.[16] Such forthrightness of speech was quite untypical of the general. The venue and the audience explain why in an improvised address he departed from his usual restraint.[17]

We find further expression of his faith and convictions in his correspondence, in letters to relatives to whom he pledged his prayers or to writers or theologians for sending him copies of their work. Although de Gaulle never went into lengthy explanations on the subject, one senses that for him religion was not extraneous to the world, nor was the world the domain of evil. In a letter to Father Carré he wrote: 'For the world of men, the world of strife, there is the Father of Salvation and peace, today as always, and nothing else'.[18] What man does in this world must be dedicated to God. Before Elizabeth de Miribel was due to take the veil, the general wrote to her: 'You will bring to God, not just yourself but an undertaking in which you had a great and noble part, whose flame will burn forever, even on our graves'.[19] How can one understand these extraordinary words otherwise than as a dedication to God of the history of the Free French by de Gaulle's former collaborator, on the eve of her becoming a Carmelite nun? It is surely legitimate to see in all this

---

[15] To the French Canadians, on 1 August 1940. Later, on 2 April 1941, in *Le Journal d' Egypte*, he wrote: 'I am a free Frenchman, I believe in God and in the love of my country'.

[16] C. de Gaulle, *Discours et messages* (Plon, Paris, 1970), Vol. 5, pp.178–9.

[17] Recalled by René Brouillet, then French ambassador to the Vatican.

[18] De Gaulle, *Lettres, notes et carnets*, 24 June 1965.

[19] Letter of 19 July 1949, in E. de Miribel, *La Liberté souffre violence* (Plon, Paris, 1981), p.221.

something of the spirituality of de Gaulle's Jesuit teachers which is far removed from the pessimistic Jansenist vision of the world usually imputed to the general. By the same token, it would also be wrong to call him a Christian traditionalist. He rejoiced in the Second Vatican Council whose importance he immediately understood and whose significance he stressed when he met Pope Paul VI on 31 May 1967. On the other hand, it is probable that he did not appreciate some of the subsequent excesses. Little wonder, either, that he remained attached to the use of Latin in the liturgy, while not questioning the use of French introduced after Vatican II.[20] At his funeral in the small church of Colombey, the ceremony was conducted in French.

The Christian flame in history

In many of his most profound and serious commitments, Charles de Gaulle turned to his deep religious faith for inspiration, a faith which was so inseparable from his patriotic feelings that there has sometimes been a tendency to look no further for his motivation. For de Gaulle, Free France was a spiritual adventure. The choice of the cross of Lorraine as his emblem symbolized the fact that, whatever the personal and individual convictions of the Free French, they were fighting for a set of essentials at the heart of which were Christian values. In an address to the American people from Radio Brazzaville on 14 July 1941, Charles de Gaulle condemned Nazism: 'On the pretext of a new order, Hitler is using terror, corruption and propaganda to force men to accept the souls of slaves, even to the point of abjuring God'.[21] The fundamentally anti-Christian nature of Nazi totalitarianism is here brought out in an extremely lucid manner.

In a message addressed on 11 March 1941 to Mira Benenson's *Glaive de l' Esprit*, the monthly publication of the French section of the 'Sword of the Spirit' movement presided over by Cardinal Hinsley, de Gaulle wrote that 'French priests, like the faithful, know that the swastika claims to rival the cross of Christ and that a victory by Hitler would plunge us back into the darkness of paganism'.[22] These words are a direct echo of Pope Pius XI's famous declaration in 1938 denouncing a cross that was the 'enemy of the cross of Christ'.[23] De Gaulle went on to say that French Catholics 'have engraved in their hearts the condemnation of Nazi heresies which the Supreme Pontiff has pronounced repeatedly and which the bishops had read out in all our churches', thus showing his knowledge of pontifical documents, such as the *Mit brennender Sorge* of 1937,

[20] As recalled by Colonel Desgrées de Lou.
[21] De Gaulle, *Discours et messages*, Vol. 1, pp.93–4.
[22] Quoted in full in Fumet, *Histoire de Dieu*, p.504.
[23] Declaration of May 1938, at the time of the meeting between Hitler and Mussolini.

or the 1938 texts on racism, and also proving that these were more widely circulated than is sometimes said.

The great speeches of the Free French period, such as the Oxford address of 25 November 1941, are deeply rooted in the social teachings of Popes Pius XI and Pius XII. The rejection of mechanized civilization, of the age of the masses, of totalitarianism, the search for a third way between liberalism and collectivism – such themes are all in keeping with the broad tendencies of social Catholicism, and more particularly with the ideas of the Thomist philosopher Jacques Maritain, the author of *Humanisme intégral*. The deep admiration which de Gaulle felt for Maritain is well recorded, as is his wish to see him join the Free French before finally convincing him to accept the Vatican Embassy in 1945.[24] In London, de Gaulle showed his sympathy for the monthly review *Volontaire pour La Cité chrétienne*, of which the moving spirits were two of Maritain's close associates, Francis Louis Closon and Maurice Schumann, both linked to the weekly *Temps présent* , as was de Gaulle himself.

It is reasonable to imagine that de Gaulle owed to Maritain the vision of a new, non-clerical Christian world which he referred to on a number of occasions. It was this which he evoked in the last dramatic days of 1944, in persuading Jacques Maritain to accept his diplomatic appointment to the Holy See. 'He asked me for this sacrifice', wrote Maritain, 'in order to accomplish something great in the cause of France; to make them understand that France is, today, the Christian world. His insistence was not brutal, but imbued with a deep and unshakeable conviction. I could not to see how I could refuse.'[25]

A few months later, on 10 May 1945, the new ambassador, whose nomination met with some resistance owing to the controversies surrounding his work, was received at the Vatican. His reply to Pius XII directly echoed de Gaulle. He portrayed France as 'one of the leading hopes of this truly human, truly universal civilization, of this Christian world, this Christendom to call it by its Christian name, to whose new flowering, directly or indirectly, all men of good will aspire today'.[26] The term 'Christendom' did not indicate a return to a political and religious system inherited from the Middle Ages, but rather the inspiration distilled from Christian values in a plan for civilization with which non-Christians could also identify. Such was the meaning given to the word by de Gaulle.

De Gaulle never stopped emphasizing the importance of Christian values in the history of France. In his radio address of 8 June 1951, on the eve of the general election, he called on 'all the spiritual families which,

[24] See *Cahiers Jacques Maritain*, 16–17 (1988).
[25] Letter to Abbé Charles Journet, in *Cahiers Jacques Maritain*, p.57.
[26] In *Documentation Catholique*, 10 June 1945, pp.421–3.

century after century, have instilled into the nation either the spirit of Christianity, or the passion for social justice, or the love of freedom, or respect for our traditions'. Over a year earlier, speaking at the Vélodrome d'Hiver, he referred to the 'three burning torches which in turn illuminate the history of France', the Christian flame 'being the one that spreads the light of love and brotherhood over the vale of human travail, the one that for century after century rekindled the spiritual inspiration of France'.[27] He further defined the meaning of these sweeping terms to the activists of the RPF, explaining that 'we are a Christian country, this is a fact, and we have been so for a very long time. We have been more or less, and more rather than less, shaped by this influence. We should not ignore this in ourselves but should recognize that all that is most human and moral in the Christian spirit is part of us.'[28] In these words, de Gaulle emphasized in his own particular fashion that the Christian tradition was inseparable from the history of France. Thus de Gaulle, a keen reader of Péguy who in the darkest hours of the Free French exalted the memory of Joan of Arc, the 'girl from Lorraine', rejected a narrow conception of a secularism which would deny the Christian tradition. After the war, he knew that agnostics and non-believers were joining the ranks of the RPF, but he felt that they could not be offended by references to the Christian tradition since in his eyes this was identified with truly human values. The France of Christianity and the France of the Rights of Man were, for de Gaulle, inseparable.

A Christian and a politician.

An outline of de Gaulle's religious convictions is the necessary prelude to a brief account of his religious politics. It is not intended to look at the latter for their own sake and in all their detail, from the Free French to the Fifth Republic. What is important is to identify de Gaulle's essential orientations and options. From the founding of the Free French, de Gaulle was concerned with the attitude of the episcopacy towards the Vichy regime. In a secret letter to Monsignor Saliège, the Archbishop of Toulouse, on 27 May 1942, he spoke of the 'alarm' he felt 'as a Christian and a Frenchman' – a remarkable association – in the face of 'the attitude, even if it was sometimes only an appearance, adopted publicly by a part of the French episcopacy towards politics and the so-called men of Vichy'. Fearing 'grave consequences for the situation of the clergy and perhaps even for religion in France after the Liberation', he wished that 'the bishops would speak loudly and clearly while there was still time so that the people of France might shake off the impression that there

[27] De Gaulle, *Discours et Messages*, 11 February 1950.
[28] De Gaulle, *Lettres, notes et carnets*, February 1950, speech to RPF representatives in Saint-Maurice.

exists a kind of solidarity between the clergy and the people who have proclaimed, accepted and aggravated the defeat of France'.[29]

The warning conveyed by these words had no official significance. It should, however, be noted that the letter was not brought to Monsignor Saliège by any ordinary messenger, but by none other than Francis-Louis Closon, sent to occupied France by the Interior Commission of the Free French. By thus approaching a prelate whose influence and feelings about Vichy were well-known, the leader of the Free French, sure that he would have to assume the responsibility of power after the Liberation, in effect addressed the French bishops as a whole and warned them to keep their distance from Vichy.

Another lesser-known episode deserves to be mentioned here. Following his arrival in Algeria and the setting up of the French Committee of National Liberation, de Gaulle conveyed his intentions to Archbishop Leynaud of Algiers.[30] The archbishop in turn informed Pius XII of the general's plans, which were seen as 'favourable to the Church'; the general used the opportunity to inform the archbishop of the appointment of communist ministers to the government and to get his reaction to the possible inclusion of Monsignor Hincky, a curate from Colmar who had taken refuge in Algeria.[31]

The visits made by de Gaulle to Pius XII and the Secretary of State, Cardinal Maglione, in the wake of the liberation of Rome, as related in the *War Memoirs*, testify to his desire as President of the GPRF to secure recognition of his legitimacy by the Holy See, which had maintained diplomatic relations with Vichy to the end. It is well known that following the liberation of France, de Gaulle refused to allow the Papal Nuncio in Vichy to continue representing the Vatican, a measure which applied to all diplomats.[32] This decision did not stop de Gaulle from paying signal homage to the former Nuncio, Monsignor Valerio Valeri.[33] In the end, after some delay in accepting the need to appoint a new Nuncio, Rome named Monsignor Roncalli, the Papal delegate in Ankara, and later Pope John XXII. The choice was not, as some have alleged without proof, a snub for General de Gaulle but rather testified to the Vatican's desire to appoint an unusual, but highly experienced diplomat to the Paris post.[34]

---

[29] A facsimile copy of this letter was published for the first time in F.-L. Closon, *Le Temps des passions. De Jean Moulin à la Libération, 1943–1944* (Presses de la Cité, Paris, 1974), p.278. It subsequently appeared in de Gaulle, *Lettres, notes et carnets*.

[30] In *Actes et documents du Saint-Siège sur la deuxième guerre mondiale*, Vol. 11, p.310. The letter of Monsignor Leynaud to Pius XII is dated 16 May 1944.

[31] Before the war, he had been linked to an anti-autonomist movement called Action Populaire Nationale d' Alsace.

[32] Father Blet, 'Pie XII et la France en guerre', *Revue d' histoire de l' Eglise en France*, July–December 1983.

[33] As recalled by René Brouillet.

[34] G. Alberigo, ed., *Jean XXIII devant l' histoire* (Seuil, Paris, 1989).

While being received by Monsignor Maglione, de Gaulle had deplored the attitude of 'certain ecclesiastical circles'.[35] One particular episode symbolizes the relationship that existed between the provisional government and the episcopacy, the banning of Cardinal Suhard from attending the ceremonies in Notre-Dame at the liberation of Paris. This decision was prompted by Catholic resistance fighters who were particularly angry at the cardinal's presence at the funeral of Vichy's information minister, Philippe Henriot, in the early summer of 1944.[36] De Gaulle took full responsibility for this decision, as he explained shortly afterwards to Monsignor Théas, Bishop of Montauban, and recounted in his *War Memoirs*. He judged it 'inadmissible' that the prelate should preside over such a ceremony, shortly after officiating at Philippe Henriot's funeral.

The historian André Latreille, then in charge of religious affairs in the provisional government, has given a definitive account both as historian and witness of the 'purge' of the episcopacy.[37] This shows that whatever the severity of de Gaulle's judgement of certain bishops, he was infinitely less exacting than the leaders of the MRP, and particularly the Minister for Foreign Affairs, Georges Bidault. In the end, an agreement was reached between Rome and Paris which led to the resignation of seven bishops from France and the overseas territories, a symbolic measure accepted by the head of the Provisional Government.[38]

In the months that followed the liberation of France, the relationship with the Catholic Church was understandably not at the forefront of de Gaulle's preoccupations. But shortly thereafter arose the question of the subsidies for private schools. In March 1945, the Consultative Assembly requested a return to the situation of 1939 and the abolition of the subsidies introduced by the Vichy government. The Minister for Education, René Capitant, re-established the status quo in the autumn of 1945. He was still hopeful, however, of finding a general solution capable of defusing this question, when the work of the Assembly and government came to a sudden end. Conscious of the political constraints on a solution re-establishing subsidies, de Gaulle did not think it wise to engage in confrontation with the secularist camp.[39] As a Roman Catholic, himself educated in religious schools, he would not tolerate any pressure from Rome on this question. When Monsignor Roncalli showed him a map of France indicating in red the number of Catholic schools destined

[35] C. de Gaulle, *War Memoirs* , Vol 2, *Unity, 1942–1944* (Weidenfeld & Nicolson, London, 1959), p. 236

[36] Closon, *Le Temps des passions.*

[37] A. Latreille, *De Gaulle, la Libération et l' Eglise catholique* (Editions du Cerf, Paris, 1978).

[38] The Archbishop of Aix-en-Provence, the Bishops of Arras and Mende, the Auxiliary Bishop of Paris, and the Apostolic Vicars of Rabat, St. Pierre et Miquelon, and Dakar.

[39] As recalled by René Brouillet.

for closure because of insufficient funding, he replied: 'this map is the map of France, it is therefore up to the French, and not a foreign authority, to make the decisions'.[40]

This principle sheds light on the attitude adopted by de Gaulle during the preparatory stages of the Debré Act on private education of December 1959. He rejected the attempts of the Fourth Republic to solve the question by an agreement with Rome, considering it a purely French matter.[41] He fully approved his Prime Minister's efforts to find a formula which, without infringing the secular nature of state schools, would establish contractual links with private schools. Pressure groups from the private school system as well as part of the Catholic hierarchy were initially extremely reticent.[42] De Gaulle's determination overcame these difficulties. He found support from Cardinal Feltin, who placed his full authority behind the compromise reached.[43]

In this affair, de Gaulle demonstrated his concern to respect the openly secular nature of the public service. From the very beginnings of the Fifth Republic, he defended article 2 of the Constitution which claims that France is a secular republic. Certain Catholic circles which remained faithful to a tradition of intransigence, were offended. To Cardinal Grente, Archbishop of Le Mans, who had informed him of his concern, he remarked with some humour: 'unless the state is ecclesiastical, I cannot see – and neither, I am sure, can your Eminence – how it can be anything but secular'.[44] But, he added, 'the whole question is knowing how, and in what spirit, it is to be secular. For it to be secular in the right way, I really think it should receive the baptism of the Church of France'. Such a notion could not but evoke, for a man with de Gaulle's upbringing, the baptism of Clovis in Reims, one of the foundations of national history. It also conjured up the dream dear to the hearts of Christian Democrats since the nineteenth century, of a 'baptised' democracy. Here again one sees the influence of Maritain's vision of a democracy which derives its strength from Christian values.

For de Gaulle, as for Tocqueville, a democratic state needed spiritual values, and he felt accordingly that it should not be indifferent to religious questions, in the interest of the nation itself. The state was thus compelled by its own mission to have a religious policy and could not remain unaffected by its relationship with the religious denominations, and first among them the Catholic Church. This attitude has at times been wrongly labelled 'Gallican', when it adopts none of the theology of

---

[40] Teitgen, *Faites entrer le témoin suivant*, p.158.
[41] As recalled by René Brouillet.
[42] 'General de Gaulle does not need your advice', he told Edouard Lizpop, the co-ordinator of the Association of Catholic Parents.
[43] As recalled by Father Wenger.
[44] De Gaulle, *Lettres, notes et carnets*, 17 September 1958, p.86.

Gallicanism and is, in reality, the attitude of the leader of a secular state. Yet de Gaulle never lost interest in religious matters. It is worth noting that in his various trips to the regions, he never failed to meet the representatives of the religious authorities, including the local bishop. He ensured that the right of the Republic since 1921 to vet politically the appointment of bishops did not become obsolete. On 17 September 1962, he wrote that it was important to 'completely reorganize the conduct of religious affairs in order to give the government real control over episcopal appointments. The Vatican appoints bishops after consulting us, but the terms and conditions are such that it is a fiction'.[45] He reiterated his concern on 29 November 1962, after receiving a letter on the subject. He wished to be better informed of Rome's intentions. He also wanted the Ministry of the Interior and prefects to be more familiar with the candidates likely to be promoted bishop. Was he in favour of a new concordat? This would be claiming too much, but he did wish the state to exercise the rights and prerogatives which it had in religious affairs, while respecting the secular basis of the state, rather than retreating into abstention and reciprocal ignorance.

In the wake of Vatican II, de Gaulle questioned Edmond Michelet (the Christian Democrat former resister to whom he entrusted missions concerning church–state relations) about the future use in the mass of certain Latin phrases relating to the Republic, which survived from the days of the concordat in the areas of France exempt from the separation of church and state in 1905.[46] 'For the state, and I think for the church as well, something important is at stake here', he remarked. This shows the importance that de Gaulle attached to church–state co-operation, with the state receiving the support of the church, and the church showing not only its loyalty to the established powers but also its concern for civil society by praying for the Republic. Far from being a new form of Gallicanism, de Gaulle's attitude testified to his conviction that the separation of church and state should be a separation in harmony.

As a statesman, Charles de Gaulle had to meet the tragic choices necessitated by political action. He had to confront the reality of violence, notably over the question of the death penalty. As head of state, he had to decide on pleas for pardon or clemency. He refused some, thus appearing inhuman.[47] He accepted seemingly unnatural political alliances such as the appointment of communist ministers or the alliance with the Soviet Union. Already, before the war, he justified the Franco-Soviet pact in a letter to his mother. 'We cannot afford to reject Russian help', he wrote on 20 November 1936, 'no matter how much we detest their

[45] De Gaulle, *Lettres, notes et carnets*, pp.250 and 276.
[46] As recalled by René Brouillet; De Gaulle, *Lettres, notes et carnets*, 30 April 1965.
[47] As recalled by Father Limague in his obituary in *La Croix*, 11 November 1970.

regime.' It was the old story of François I allied with the Muslims against Emperor Charles V.

It is important to ask the question of what the secularization of modern politics meant for de Gaulle. He did not equate it with indifference to the rights of individuals nor with contempt for the principles and values which inform political action. De Gaulle was attached to such principles and values, which is why the reference to Machiavelli which is so often made in relation to him is without foundation.[48] For him, the secularization of politics was an affirmation of the state's independence in its own sphere. This suggests Richelieu rather than Machiavelli. In his *Testament Politique* (the 1947 edition of which features an introduction written by a loyal Gaullist, Léon Noël), Richelieu denied having given in to reasons of state, claiming instead to have tried to remain faithful to the rights of individuals and to natural morality in his politics. But he drew a distinction between secular and religious interests, not hesitating to ally himself with the German Protestant princes against the Habsburgs. An early eighteenth-century Jesuit, Father Lallemant, wondered about this seemingly scandalous alliance of Catholic princes 'with heretics'.[49] He suggested 'that God might derive great benefits from it which are hidden from us. We should not condemn the conduct of our princes nor that of our ministers, but leave God to act, and wait patiently and silently until events occur which Providence will ensure celebrate His glory'. But this spirit of resignation in the face of divine will suggested correspondingly that the political world enjoyed its own autonomy and that, on the whole, one could not derive a course of political conduct from holy scripture.

To return to de Gaulle. He doubtless considered that a statesman in the secular world of politics should make choices according to his conscience. He took exception to political evangelism yet was deeply influenced and motivated by moral imperatives. Ambassador P. L. Blanc recalls in a moving testimony that de Gaulle 'asked himself if he was right not only politically but also morally'.[50] On the base of the cross of Lorraine memorial to de Gaulle at Colombey-les-Deux Eglises is the inscription: 'In our time, the only battle worth fighting is the battle for man. Man must be saved, must be allowed to live and develop'. This expresses the fundamental conviction which guided Charles de Gaulle, as a Christian statesman, through the obstacles and dramas of his political existence.

---

[48] Machiavelli contrasted Christian ethics with pagan ethics, which he saw as a source of energy and strength. He deplored the 'weakened state of the world caused by the present religion' (A. Renaudet, *Machiavel* [Gallimard, Paris, 1956], p.87). There is obviously nothing akin to this idea in Charles de Gaulle.

[49] Quoted by Joseph Lecler, *The Two Sovereignties. A Study of the Relationship between the Church and State* (1946; English translation: Burns, Oates & Washbourne, London, 1952).

[50] P.L. Blanc, *De Gaulle au soir de sa vie* (Fayard, Paris, 1990), p.206.

8

De Gaulle and Gaullism in the Fifth Republic

Serge Berstein

When de Gaulle came to power in June 1958, nobody knew what political line he was going to follow, or what Gaullism really stood for. Indeed, ever since de Gaulle had erupted on to the scene of French history in 1940, Gaullism had taken two very different – if not incompatible – forms. One was the Gaullism of the resistance movement, which sought consensus and unity, trying to transcend the divisions created by war and to forge the golden legend of a nation that had been united behind the provisional government to drive out the occupying forces. The second was the political and opposition-oriented Gaullism of the Fourth Republic's bitter enemy, the RPF, which failed to recover the inspiration of Free France, in the absence of the outbreak of a third world war that de Gaulle had believed to be imminent. However, throughout these two periods, Gaullism did present one constant and distinctive feature, which allowed the French to appreciate its true nature in 1958. This was a constant concern with the greatness of France, which demanded above all else a revision of its institutions, something which de Gaulle had made his permanent battle theme from 1945 to 1958. This was why, in 1958, Gaullism appeared first and foremost as a factor in the destruction of the traditional republican model.

De Gaulle and Gaullism as factors in the destruction of the traditional republican model

At the end of the Fourth Republic, a majority of the general public and of the French political world were still attached to the republican model which had been devised in the late nineteenth and early twentieth centuries.

This model, a legacy of the battles fought against the republic's opponents at the end of the nineteenth century, and consolidated by the confrontations which had occurred around the time of the Dreyfus affair, presented itself as an overall system or 'world model' for the organization of society. It had its philosophical roots in the rationalist legacy of the eighteenth century and a concomitant concern with the secular state and educational system. Its historical references had their source in the epic of the French Revolution and its nineteenth-century sequels. Finally, its institutional ideal and social vision were presented as the fulfilment of the promises held out by the French Revolution for both state and society. In the area of institutions this ideal culminated in the exaltation of the parliamentary regime, which gave institutional supremacy to the elected representatives of the people themselves, who constituted the real repositories of sovereignty. Any attempt to reinforce the power of the executive was thus seen as an attempt to return to the days of personal power, evoking shades of a Louis-Napoleon Bonaparte or a General Boulanger, both alien to the republican tradition. Finally, at the social level, the republican model advocated the promotion of the most able, of the most talented and courageous, facilitated by a competitive selection process in schools which was designed to enable even the very poor to rise to the top. This ideal explains why the republic found a social base in the French middle classes which ensured its stability from the end of the nineteenth century onwards. Grafted on to France in the years before the First World War, it must have appeared more and more anachronistic as the twentieth century wore on, and was violently contested as early as the 1930s. Nevertheless, in the 1950s it was still deeply rooted in people's minds as a kind of model which could probably be improved upon, but whose basic foundations were no longer in question.[1]

Charles de Gaulle, however, did not share this view of the republican model. His family were originally monarchists, even if they rallied to the republic, and in the military circles he frequented, loyalty to the republic was seen more as a duty than a passion. As far as he was concerned, the republic was an established institutional system which there was no reason to oppose, as long as it guaranteed the greatness of the country. It corresponded to the current state of French mores and customs, and in the absence of an outmoded monarchy, it was a type of regime that could be lived with. For de Gaulle, however, loyalty to its principles did not imply any particular allegiance to its philosophical roots, its historical references or to the institutional parliamentary system which epitomized the republican spirit. His comments in the speech that he made at Bayeux in 1946 are very revealing in this respect. In advocating a

---

[1] S. Berstein and O. Rudelle, eds., *Le modèle républicain* (Presses Universitaires de France, Paris, 1992).

regime in which the head of state would be the institutional keystone, and in which the prerogatives of Parliament would be reduced to legislative and budgetary roles, de Gaulle was merely offering what he saw as sensible comment, based on the idea that in order to avoid a return to a crisis like that of 1940, the nation had to have a strong state capable of defending the general interest. There was nothing sacred about institutions. They were simply the mechanism, and a dispensable one at that, by which at any given time the nation ensured its capacity to respond to the problems of the day. In the eyes of the traditional republicans, however, this amounted to querying the entire historical heritage on which the republican model was founded, and as far as most republicans were concerned de Gaulle's campaign was aimed at acquiring personal power. This revived all the old phantoms of Bonapartism and Boulangism and, for communists, the ghost of Fascism.[2]

Under these circumstances, it was understandable that de Gaulle's return to power should have caused great alarm in the republican camp. Yet the crisis of May–June 1958 showed that, although the defence of the republican model remained essential for most people in the political world, the general public did not seem to share their concern. The teachers' strike and the demonstration held at *Place de la République* on 29 May 1958 showed no evidence of any genuine mass uprising in defence of the regime of the Fourth Republic. Yet politicians retained their doubts, and at the press conference that he gave on 19 May 1958 de Gaulle was asked straight out whether he was seeking a dictatorship. Before conferring him with full powers, the leaders of the Fourth Republic – and specifically Guy Mollet – made him undertake to maintain the parliamentary regime and to retain a Chamber of Deputies in which seats were filled by open elections.[3] Did this amount to saying that Gaullism was preparing to fit into the mould of a republican model which had proved to be unworkable, even in the hands of its own supporters? If some of those who participated in the drafting of the Constitution, such as the socialist Guy Mollet, were inclined to think so, future events would quickly show how mistaken they were.

The new Constitution presented to the French people on 4 September 1958, and adopted by referendum on 28 September, incorporated a rigorous separation of powers and established a mixed regime in France that constitutional lawyers were to describe as 'semi-presidential'. On the one hand, it maintained a parliamentary regime, because the government was still answerable to the National Assembly. On the other, it made the head of state the institutional keystone of the system. No longer

[2] S. Courtois and M. Lazar, eds., *50 ans d'une passion française – De Gaulle et les communistes* (Balland, Paris, 1991).
[3] R. Rémond, *1958: Le retour de de Gaulle* (Editions Complexe, Bruxelles, 1983), and O. Rudelle, *Mai 1958, de Gaulle et la République* (Plon, Paris, 1988).

elected by parliament, but by an enlarged electoral college of 80, 000 *notables*, he now enjoyed extended powers which put him in complete control of the executive branch of government. He could nominate the Prime Minister and members of the government, he presided over meetings of the Council of Ministers and was responsible for the promulgation of laws. Most importantly of all, he now had three powers at his disposal which enabled him to play a leading role in political life. He could call a referendum to decide the fate of any legislative proposal which would affect the republic's political institutions, he had the right to dissolve the National Assembly, and in the event that the territorial integrity of the republic, its institutions or its ability to carry out its international obligations were threatened, the head of state could assume special powers under article 16 of the Constitution. [4]

The new Constitution, adopted by an overwhelming majority of the French electorate (almost 80 per cent of all votes cast were in its favour), finally led to the election of Charles de Gaulle as President of the Republic on 21 December 1958. Yet its early years were dominated by the unusual and extremely dramatic circumstances of the final stages of the Algerian War. Fearful of a military *putsch* which might give power to the quasi-Fascist officers of the Algerian Army, the overwhelming majority of the French public trusted de Gaulle to bring an end to the conflict. Politicians, aware that only the head of state possessed the authority necessary to break the deadlock, reluctantly had to leave him a free hand. Under these circumstances, de Gaulle was able to act as he saw fit and to put his presidential powers into practice, even extending them considerably beyond the parameters laid down by the text adopted in September 1958. Considering himself as the only person authorized to interpret the Constitution, addressing the nation over the head of the Assembly during visits, speeches and press conferences, and calling referenda to endorse his policies whenever necessary, he appeared to reduce the government's role to one of simply implementing his policies, and the role of Parliament to simply drafting the texts necessary for putting those policies into effect. This impression perhaps needs to be qualified to a certain extent, but it was none the less essentially accurate. In this way, de Gaulle transformed the President of the Fifth Republic into a temporary monarch, answerable only to the will of the people as expressed in a series of referenda which allowed him to renew his democratic legitimacy. In September 1962, when he completed and clarified the institutional structure of the Fifth Republic by proposing that the head of state be elected by universal suffrage, he may have been able to claim that he was being consistent with the practice of election that he had first

[4] O. Duhamel and J.-L. Parodi, eds., *La Constitution de la Ve République* (Presses de la Fondation Nationale des Sciences Politiques, Paris, 1965).

instituted in 1958. Nevertheless, there is no doubt that he was diluting the concessions that he had been forced to make to the leaders of the various political parties then, and the reservations expressed by Michel Debré, along with the protests of Guy Mollet or Pierre Pflimlin, showed that supporters of the republican tradition felt they had been cheated. However, these protests soon began to look like a rearguard action in the context of 1962. The regime had evolved towards a strengthening of presidential powers, and although this prompted all political groups, except the Gaullists of the UNR, to come together within the *cartel des non* – or to adopt the same position outside it in the case of the communists – public opinion did not support them. By a clear majority of 61.75 per cent the French people solemnly ratified the destruction of the traditional republican model, which had already been severely weakened in 1958.[5]

This was how Gaullism first showed its face under the Fifth Republic – as a strong state dominated by an all-powerful president whose power came directly from the general will of the people and who was responsible to no one else. Nothing could be more different from the republican model. For in this the limitation of executive power – monitored, controlled and kept in its place by the elected government – was regarded as the only effective guarantee of the freedom of the citizen. This strengthening of the state was obviously designed to allow the nation to confront and to resolve the problems that it faced. Yet, over the years, its exercise of this power was to reveal the nature of Gaullism and its contribution to history.

De Gaulle and the exercise of power: the nature of Gaullism

In the course of his political activities, de Gaulle never claimed to draw his inspiration from any particular doctrine or theory. He left behind no writings which might help to define Gaullism as a political ideology. At the very most one can try to extrapolate a tentative definition of the nature of Gaullism from his specific stances on various problems that he had to deal with. Using this approach, however, one is quickly forced to admit the obvious fact that he did not define any particular line of thought that could be used as the basis for a discussion of Gaullist doctrine. His attitude was purely pragmatic, based on *realpolitik,* and on a readiness to adapt to circumstances and to make allowances for inescapable constraints, so that he could arrive at what he considered to be the least unsatisfactory solution to any particular problem. A good example of this was the peace treaty in Algeria, where he attempted over the years

[5] S. Berstein, *La France de l'expansion, I, La République gaullienne 1958–1969* (Editions du Seuil, Paris, 1989) pp.104–114.

to work out 'the most French solution' but finally found himself obliged to negotiate with the FLN and listen to their conditions in order to achieve a peace which everyone knew offered France only very flimsy guarantees of being fulfilled.

However, even if de Gaulle's exercise of power was inspired by a pragmatism which does not allow us to define Gaullism as anything other than unconditional loyalty to the leader, at least the goal that he pursued was quite clear. It consisted of the 'certain idea of France' referred to in the opening lines of the *War Memoirs*. France, for him, was an almost mystical entity which could not be defined simply in terms of its national territory or its inhabitants. The struggle that de Gaulle led was in the service of this entity and of his particular conception of it: one full of greatness, beauty and generosity. Moreover, as he saw it, it was vital to use every means available to make France's voice heard in the world, to defend its interests, to ensure that it was respected: in short, to ensure that it fulfilled its destiny, which was of far greater importance than that of any group or individual within it. This means that de Gaulle's world vision was based on French nationalism and was at odds with the republican belief in the defence of the rights of the individual against reason of state. Nevertheless, his form of nationalism was closer to that of the French revolutionary tradition than to that of the nationalist right, and his idea of France permeated all his policies, without elevating any one of them into an overriding dogma.[6]

Once his goal had been clearly defined, the means of achieving it were many and varied, but all of them drew their inspiration from this founding idea. De Gaulle's first aim, once the Constitution had been established, was to free France from the various constraints hindering her international activities, especially those which resulted from her colonial empire. In fact, in the light of the Algerian War, it seemed evident to him that involvement in colonial warfare divided the nation, ruined its financial stability, provoked criticism of it at international level and prevented it from playing the leading world role it was destined for. Yet this realism in no way prevented him from strongly resenting the sacrifice he had to make in the name of political expediency. 'For a man of my age and experience', he wrote in his *Memoirs of Hope*, 'it was truly a cruel blow to have to be the mastermind of such a change.' It mattered little, for in 1962 de Gaulle was to extract France from the hornets' nest of Algeria. Independence was also given to thirteen other French overseas territories, once the French had become convinced that there was no alternative, and it was forcibly imposed on the army and on the French residents of Algeria, who found themselves sacrificed on the altar of political realism. By 1960, having tried to keep the Black African colonies

[6] Berstein, *La France de l'expansion*, pp.221ff.

within a French Community, he agreed to grant them independence without breaking their links to France.[7]

Once France had been extracted from her colonial problems, she had to ensure her military, political and technological independence. To this end, de Gaulle ordered a major drive in the area of military applications of nuclear research, and in 1960, with the explosion of the first French-built atomic bomb in the Sahara, made France a member of the select club of nuclear powers. This conquest of military independence was completed in 1968 by the explosion of a hydrogen bomb in Mururoa. However, the development of a nuclear arsenal would have been of little use if France had been forced to relinquish control over its use. In 1966, in order to release the country from its subordination to the United States within NATO, he decided to withdraw from the military wing of the Atlantic alliance, while remaining within its political wing. Finally, a refusal to become subject to the Americans in technology, which he regarded as the first step towards eventual economic subordination, prompted him to encourage a series of *grands projets* which met with varying success: the construction of Concorde, the SECAM colour television process, French techniques for uranium enrichment, the launch of the nuclear submarine *Le Redoutable*, the development of the Calculus Plan for the construction of computers, and so on.[8]

However, this concern with national independence was completely meaningless if France did not have the power to make her voice heard in the world. The means to achieve this, in de Gaulle's eyes, lay in financial and economic success, in the modernization of the country and the creation of a flourishing cultural life. De Gaulle paid close attention to all these areas, regarding them as real channels of power and influence, even though he had no particular theory to apply. If he was such a fervent supporter of a strong franc, it was less out of an attachment to financial orthodoxy than out of his belief in the currency as the visible sign of national economic strength. This was the reason why he supported the Pinay-Rueff plan in 1958 and complemented it with a psychological measure which was characteristic of his intentions, the creation of the revalued *franc lourd* which, replacing 100 old francs, placed the French currency on an equal footing with the deutschmark or the Swiss franc. It was also the reason why in November 1968 he firmly rejected the devaluation of the franc recommended by business circles. None the less, he was perfectly aware that the strength of the currency depended

[7] *La politique africaine du général de Gaulle (1958–1969)*, (Proceedings of the Colloquium organized by the *Centre bordelais d'études africaines*, the *Centre d'études d'Afrique noire* and the *Institut Charles de Gaulle*, Bordeaux, 20 October 1979), (Pédone, Paris, 1980).

[8] J. Doise and M. Vaisse, *Diplomatie et outil militaire, 1871–1962* (Imprimerie nationale, Paris, 1987); A. Grosser, *Affaires Exterieures. La politique étrangère de la France 1944–1984* (Flammarion, Paris, 1984).

largely on the performance of the French economy and, contrary to the legend which claims that he had no interest in economic problems (a legend maintained by the apocryphal phrase *l'intendance suivra*) he placed great emphasis on the innovative capacities and the dynamism of the French economy. It was in order to encourage them that he exposed France to international competition by speeding up the movement towards a system of free exchange within the Common Market. Convinced that the state could not afford to neglect such an essential factor of national greatness, he relied on state planning to set targets for growth and encouraged mergers and structural modernization, particularly in the leading high-technology sectors of aviation, computers and the space industry. From 1963 on, in spite of these decisions which were dictated by the concern for efficiency rather than by dogma, he allowed Valéry Giscard d'Estaing to reduce the level of state intervention and return to increasingly free market policies.[9]

If the economy was to provide France with the means to achieve power, an increase in her influence also required a flourishing cultural life. Here de Gaulle was assisted by André Malraux, his formidable Minister for Culture, who was assigned the twin duties of describing de Gaulle's actions in epic terms, and of providing a cultural equivalent to his policies for achieving greatness. The policy of restoring Paris's former splendour by cleaning up its major monuments, of opening *maisons de la culture*, and giving recognition to artists, writers and intellectuals, were all gestures designed to make de Gaulle's presidency into one of the high points of French civilization.[10]

What were the concrete results of these attempts to restore France to a position of greatness which de Gaulle believed had been lost because of the Second World War and the problems of the Fourth Republic? It is undeniable that France's prestige under the Fifth Republic was considerable, and that de Gaulle's state visits abroad attracted an audience that far surpassed what her actual power might have warranted. However, the results remained limited. De Gaulle made some successful speeches, and his prognostications were sometimes correct. But he was more of a crowd-stirrer than a decision-maker. His speech in Phnom-Penh was less influential in securing American withdrawal from Indo-China than the protests that erupted within the United States itself. The success of his South American trip achieved no tangible results, because it was soon evident that France was unable to offer any alternative to American aid. As for his speech about *Québec libre*, its only effect was to aggravate an existing problem, and he could offer only verbal encouragement to

[9] A. Prate, *Les batailles économiques du général de Gaulle* (Plon, Paris, 1978).
[10] *De Gaulle et Malraux* (Proceedings of the Colloquium organized by the *Institut Charles de Gaulle*, 13–15 November 1986) (Plon, Paris, 1987).

supporters of independence. In a nutshell, French hopes for counter-balancing American supremacy were short-lived. The needling attacks that he made on the United States certainly drew world attention to genuine problems – America's assumption of the role of world policeman, the distortions produced by an international monetary system based on the dollar, and so on. But his attempt to counter-balance the weight of the United States by strengthening ties with the USSR or by encouraging the states of Eastern Europe to distance themselves from their Soviet protectors in the same way as France was doing from the United States, both came to dead ends. Most importantly of all, his wish to give France the means of playing a major role in the world, through the construction of a European political dimension based on a Franco-German axis, was frustrated. France's EEC partners rejected the idea of a political Europe cut off from the United States and excluding the United Kingdom, and Chancellor Adenauer's successors were to set about doing everything possible to dilute any political substance there might have been to the agreements that he and de Gaulle had signed. So we arrive at the paradox whereby General de Gaulle had effectively given France the means to achieve relative independence and had restored her initiative in international matters, but had failed to achieve his goal of restoring the country's status as a great world power. Most of all, intent as he was on pursuing the politics of greatness, he had failed to notice the divide which gradually opened up after 1962, isolating the leadership of the country from popular aspirations. [11]

The limits of Gaullism

In his obsession with the greatness of France, de Gaulle ascribed only secondary importance to the various aspirations of French society towards increased consumer spending, greater self-esteem or the defence of sectional interests. A man of duty himself, he did not see the state's function in terms of catering for a growing aspiration towards greater material comforts. Instead, he saw national destiny as the only thing worthy of his attention, and felt certain that the real stakes in the world were being played for on the chessboard of international relations. Consequently, a split gradually developed between de Gaulle and the French public, which was reflected in contemporary opinion polls. Confident in the power that he had gained through referenda and the ballot box, he imperiously displayed his intention of participating in major international decisions, while a significant proportion of the population grew increasingly uneasy with a style of leadership that

[11] Berstein, *La France de L'expansion*, pp.267–73

appeared distant from them, and unconcerned with the concrete aspirations of the French people.

This conflict emerged in the early 1960s, with the thorny question of how the benefits of economic growth were to be distributed. The farmers' protest movements of 1960 and 1961, marked by road blocks and by the occupation of the sub-prefecture in Morlaix, the great miners' strike of 1963, the discontent of small shopkeepers and tradesmen who came together to form the CID-UNATI in the late 1960s, and the increased number of strikes in the civil service were all symptomatic of the discontent felt by social groups which, because of their status or economic change, had gained little from growing prosperity. On to this permanent backdrop of social gloom were soon thrown the vague aspirations for recognition and personal fulfilment felt by the new social groups created by the rapid urbanization of France. But de Gaulle had no real answer to this social malaise. In the days of the RPF he had called for the association of capital and labour, and he still seemed attached to the idea. But in 1965, when Louis Vallon had a law passed by the National Assembly providing for profit-sharing amongst employees, he allowed his Prime Minister, Georges Pompidou, to convince him that the measure was premature, and it was shelved.[12]

Another emerging social group that the Gaullists had failed to notice was youth, which was becoming a distinct social group. They were now a specific group of consumers, with their own means of self-expression, recognizable codes of dress and speech, and a specific culture of their own; and they found little they could identify with in a leadership which they saw as traditional, stiff-necked, and light years away from their own preoccupations. The whirlwind events of May 1968 were to be an abrupt revelation of their existence. Combined with the social malaise already noted above, this whirlwind was to trigger off the most serious crisis faced by any French government since 1945, and it came very close to toppling the regime. In a subsequent analysis of the nature of the divide which had sprung up between himself and French society, de Gaulle offered participation as a solution to the crisis. But this came too late to be effective, especially as those to whom the offer was addressed had little or no confidence in the leadership proposing it.[13]

But just when Gaullism was suffering the effects of this crisis in society, it was to be let down by a third group, that of the *notables* – local representatives, and leading figures in economic and political life – none of whom had been natural supporters of de Gaulle. These key figures naturally supported the established structures, and their status brought

[12] J. L. Monneron and A. Rowley, *Les 25 ans qui ont transformé la France* (Nouvelle Librairie de France, Paris, 1986).
[13] 'Mai 68', *Pouvoirs*, 39, 1986.

with it an inherent conservatism. They had always looked upon Gaullism warily when it put itself forward as a force for modernization in French society, with the objective of overturning obsolete structures. This had been evident during the war years, when the *notables* had opted for Vichy and had only reluctantly come out in favour of Gaullism in 1943 or 1944. The same was true of the period of the RPF, when they had seen de Gaulle as potentially disruptive of the stability that had returned after the war. The *notables* rallied to de Gaulle in 1958 out of a concern for order and a fear of civil war, but they gradually distanced themselves from him after 1962. They were prevented from coming out openly against him through fear of the political vacuum that his departure would have caused, but the crisis of 1968 fuelled their hostility and reassured them that a potential successor was available. Alarmed by the plans for participation which de Gaulle subsequently made the main plank of his political programme, they were appalled at being prevented from using devaluation to compensate for the salary rises they had been forced to concede in 1968. Neither did they accept Jean-Marcel Jeanneney's plans for constitutional reform, which proposed a fundamental transformation of the Senate and the loss of its decision-making capacity. They no longer had to worry about a political vacuum, for the atmosphere of panic which had followed the May uprising had produced a conservative landslide in the legislative elections of June and opponents of de Gaulle's reform proposals could now find a natural leader in the former Prime Minister, Georges Pompidou. During the events of May, he had shown great presence of mind, firmness and statesmanlike qualities. Reassured by this, the *notables* were to add their voices to those of the opposition and vote 'no' in the April 1969 referendum, thereby forcing de Gaulle from power.[14] So, in 1969, de Gaulle fell foul of the very system of universal suffrage which he had used as the source of his authority.

The legacy of Gaullism: a new republican model

De Gaulle's departure from power, his withdrawal from political life, and his death on November 1970 were thought by most people at the time to mean the end of Gaullism. But was this really the case? One might have thought so when de Gaulle was replaced by Georges Pompidou, a more traditional statesman than the founding father of the Fifth Republic, especially when one considers the care with which he pursued a policy designed to open the political spectrum to include the very *notables* who had played such an important role in de Gaulle's downfall. Following the neo-Gaullism incarnated by Georges Pompidou, the

[14] S. Berstein, *Les notables et le général de Gaulle*, paper presented at the Colloquium on 'Les droites et le général de Gaulle', Nice, January 1990.

presidency subsequently passed to the school of neo-liberalism led by Valéry Giscard d'Estaing – who was not a Gaullist – and then to various shades of socialism under the guiding hand of François Mitterrand, who throughout the duration of the Fifth Republic had been de Gaulle's sworn enemy. Between 1986 and 1988, when Jacques Chirac became Prime Minister, as leader of the RPR party which had replaced the UDR in 1976, it was difficult to discern any trace in his policies of the Gaullism that he claimed as his inspiration.

So, did Gaullism die with Charles de Gaulle? If one takes the term to refer to the pragmatic political practices that de Gaulle had followed in certain given situations, then the answer is undoubtedly yes. Since circumstances had changed, the policies pursued necessarily had to evolve with them. But the same may not be true if one considers the true essence of Gaullism, namely the primacy accorded to this 'certain idea of France' that he consistently referred to, and the means of making it a reality with the help of a strong state, capable of forging a national unity that could override domestic political disagreements. In this respect, successive Presidents of the Republic have tried to unite the entire French nation around great national aspirations and to achieve the kind of consensus which had been an integral part of Gaullism. This was something that de Gaulle himself was never able to achieve, because of his aloof style, his taste for dramatic situations, his combative spirit and his defiant attitude towards opponents.

For their part however, Georges Pompidou, Valéry Giscard d'Estaing and François Mitterrand all tried, with varying degrees of success, to incarnate the national unity of purpose which de Gaulle had been able to represent by virtue of his historical legitimacy and his endorsement in successive referenda. Georges Pompidou did so, passing from the politics of *ouverture* directed towards the centrists to the appeal made to 'all the others' to rally against the communists at the 1973 elections. Valéry Giscard d'Estaing, who consistently advocated the merits of *décrispation* (a more relaxed political style), looked for the same kind of consensus without ever managing to achieve it. Only François Mitterrand, who at the beginning of his first term of office had put himself forward as the champion of the left, finally managed to turn the operation to his advantage after 1984, and especially during the period of cohabitation from 1986 to 1988. For the RPR's victory in the 1986 election relieved him of the burden of day-to-day politics and enabled him to present himself as the defender of the greater national interest. In this respect, his presidential campaign of 1988 on the theme of a 'united France' achieved the Gaullist ambition of bringing the French nation together across the party divide, as well as a consensus on all major political issues which has existed ever since.[15] But it is striking that this consensus originally rested

[15] S. Berstein, 'La lutte des classes est terminée', *L'Histoire*, 143, April 1991

upon what could be called a Gaullist reading of a new republican model.

In many respects, the consensus which emerged in stages since 1969 was rooted in the founding myth of the Gaullist republic of 1958–69, to which all the successive presidents have referred for their authority. If one returns to the four elements which had served to define the republican model at the beginning of the century, it becomes apparent that the only theme missing from the list is that of the philosophical roots of the regime. Yet this absence is significant for the republican model of the early years of the century drew its inspiration from the rationalist tradition of the French left, and automatically excluded Catholics, thereby denying them a place within the republican consensus. By refusing to attach itself to any particular philosophical model, the Fifth Republic could give full rein to the ideology of a unanimous rallying of the people which was a part of its specific nature.

At the same time, however, it is not difficult to detect in Gaullism other elements of the republican model, which enabled the regime to draw on historical references. Its frame of reference was not that of the French Revolution, for this had now ceased to be seen as the turning point in world history that it had been under the Third and Fourth Republics, and despite the recent bicentenary celebrations has now almost disappeared from the history syllabus in schools. Instead the regime used as its points of historical reference the entire history of France, or at least its more spectacular periods, with a special place reserved for the Resistance, interpreted as a rallying together of the whole French nation for the purpose of driving out the occupying enemy and re-establishing its freedom. Only a handful of traitors and a few nostalgic Pétain supporters could feel excluded from this, and so de Gaulle could be seen as the rallying force and symbol of national unity.

This fundamental reference to the war years and the Resistance naturally encouraged the idea that the defence of freedom required a strong state. Putting an end to arguments over the enormous institutional power of the presidency which raged during his own lifetime, de Gaulle's death, along with the subsequent accession to presidential office of men from the other main political traditions of France, has consolidated the institutions of the Fifth Republic in most people's eyes. The alternation of power in 1981 and the period of cohabitation from 1986–8 was fundamental to this consolidation. Gaullism had therefore managed to introduce an idea into France which would have been unacceptable under the previous republics, namely that the republic was not incompatible with a strong executive. This amounted to a genuine revolution, for politicians such as Millerand, Doumergue or Tardieu, who had previously tried to put forward the idea, had been accused of Bonapartism or even Fascism. This consensus over institutions was therefore something entirely new in a country where there had always previously been a certain section of public opinion permanently opposed to the regime.

Gaullism was also responsible for the very widespread agreement reached in the area of France's foreign and defence policies. On the question of the need for a policy of national autonomy, backed up by an independent defence force spearheaded by a nuclear strike capacity, or on the need for France to be independent when it came to decisions in the area of international relations – the responsibility for which belonged to the head of state, as sole representative of the nation – de Gaulle's views were once fiercely resisted by politicians on the left and and by some of those on the right. Yet today they are more or less unanimously accepted. During the period of cohabitation between 1986 and 1988, François Mitterrand reapplied the practices of his predecessors and gained lasting acceptance for the idea that the decisions over foreign and defence policy were solely a matter for the president, with the government's responsibility being limited to putting them into effect. The widespread consensus between public opinion and the political parties on this point was further consolidated during the Gulf War, when there seemed to be almost unanimous agreement over the choices open to the president. Any disagreements were confined to minor points of detail.

Finally, the new republican model also included a social agenda, and benefited from the support of a dynamic social group. This social project, established in a pragmatic way in de Gaulle's time, took on a more concrete form under Georges Pompidou, and involved an institutionalized distribution of the fruits of economic growth. With the oil crisis of 1973 and the reduction or elimination of economic growth, the project became transformed into an appeal for national solidarity, once again institutionalized in such a way as to favour the victims of the crisis. In one shape or another, the project had the same basic aim – to bring about greater unity and national cohesion by guaranteeing the great majority of people a minimum threshold level of consumer participation. The introduction of a basic minimum income in 1988 completed the picture. This social project, which was designed to smooth over the various tensions created by the emergence of a consumer society, ensured that the new republican model enjoyed the support of middle-class wage-earners, who were both the largest social group in France and the most important supporters of the Gaullist republic. Hence they have become the archetypal citizens of the Fifth Republic, just as the small shopkeeper or tradesperson had been under the Third Republic.[16]

The creation and consolidation of this new republican model, which still exists today, can therefore be seen as representing a kind of revenge and posthumous victory for de Gaulle, and for the few simple principles

---

[16] S. Berstein, 'La Ve République, un nouveau modèle républicain', in Berstein and Rudelle eds., *Le modèle républicain*.

that he incarnated which go together to make up the essence of Gaullism. On his return to power, de Gaulle was bitterly opposed by traditionalist republicans, who looked back nostalgically to the two previous republics. He was attacked all his life as the embodiment of a detested form of personal power, and was overthrown because he had failed to convey his message to the social groups who had gained least from the years of economic growth, or because he had failed to respond to the often confused or inarticulate aspirations of the younger generation. Yet today, more than twenty years after his death, Charles de Gaulle is perceived as the inspirational force behind the republic he founded more than thirty years ago, and Gaullism is regarded as the common heritage of a French society which, for the first time in its history, has arrived at an unprecedented consensus over the fundamental principles on which it is based.

9

De Gaulle and May 1968

Julian Jackson

'I greet the year 1968 with serenity ... with satisfaction.' These words of de Gaulle at the end of 1967 are one of those ironic hostages to fortune in which historians delight. In fact, this lack of prescience was widely shared. In 1967 de Gaulle's Prime Minister, Pompidou, had declared that the government's education policy was the achievement of which he was most proud. Nor must de Gaulle's complacency be exaggerated. For several years he had been harrying his ministers of education about the need to prevent a university crisis by introducing selection. Nevertheless, it is the ironic 'serenity' that history remembers.

For de Gaulle, 1968 was a tragic history of ironies. There was the irony that, having famously called in 1945 for 'twelve million fine babies' in ten years, he should himself be so devastatingly challenged by that baby boom generation twenty-two years later. The greatest irony of all was that de Gaulle, who believed that his crowning achievement was to have created a strong state, was in 1968 confronted with a crisis in which the state was not merely challenged but seemed entirely to have disappeared. De Gaulle, who once said that 'France does not exist except by virtue of the state', was humiliatingly attacked by François Mitterrand on 28 May 1968 with the words: 'In France since the 3 May 1968, the state no longer exists'.

Mitterrand's statement was no exaggeration. To quote one of Pompidou's closest aides, Edouard Balladur, 'I had the impression, more precisely and painfully each day, that we were without power or force, as in a dream when one absolutely wants to do something but fails; one after another the instruments of authority succumbed to paralysis'.[1] On

[1] E. Balladur, *L' Arbre de mai* (Atelier Marcel Jullian, Paris, 1977), p.154.

27 May an over-eager Matignon official had to be prevented from starting to burn the archives – a haunting reminiscence of the bonfire of documents in the Quai d'Orsay on 16 May 1940 as the Germans approached.[2] De Gaulle himself saw parallels: 'In less than thirty years', he remarked at the end of his life, 'the French elite has collapsed twice: in June 1940 and in May 1968'.[3] As in 1940, so in 1968, it seemed that the state had ceased to exist as power trickled through the fingers like sand.

The narrative of the events that had led to this situation is easily summarized.[4] The events of May in France were unique among 1960s student movements because they spread to the working class, and developed into a political crisis threatening the survival of the regime. The exclusively student stage lasted from 3 to 13 May. Massive student demonstrations culminated on 10 May in the so-called 'night of the barricades' when barricades were constructed in the Latin Quarter, leading to a pitched battle with the police. The students' objectives initially centred around the release of those who had been arrested after the first demonstrations, and on the reopening of the Sorbonne which had been closed on 3 May as a security precaution, but the movement was radicalized by the violent police reaction. During this first phase of events Pompidou was away in Iran and Afghanistan, and the government's policy vacillated. After the night of the barricades, popular revulsion against the police caused the trade unions to call a demonstration and a one-day general strike on 13 May. Meanwhile Pompidou, returning on 11 May, decided to capitulate by reopening the Sorbonne. This did not prevent the 13 May demonstration from being an extraordinary success, thus sparking off phase two of the Events: the entry of the working class.

The first strikes broke out on 14 May. Two weeks later France was paralysed by the most extensive strike movement in her history. The students now receded into the background. They had occupied the reopened Sorbonne and then the Odeon but at least they were no longer in the streets: the strikers now posed the main threat. As towards the students, Pompidou was conciliatory. Although the union leaders had had little to do with the outbreak of the strikes, Pompidou hoped that they would channel the strikers' aspirations into negotiable demands. Meanwhile, on 24 May, de Gaulle, who had been on an official visit to Romania between 14 and 19 May, spoke on television. He announced that the crisis showed the need for a 'mutation' of society: people wanted greater participation in the decisions affecting their lives. He proposed a referendum on this subject, and said that if defeated he would resign. His speech

[2] Balladur, *L' Arbre de mai*, pp.303–4.
[3] P.-L. Blanc, *De Gaulle au soir de sa vie* (Fayard, Paris, 1990), p.123.
[4] There are many narratives of May 1968 of which L. Joffrin, *Mai 1968. Histoire des événements* (Seuil, Paris, 1988) is the most recent. A. Dansette, *Mai 1968* (Plon, Paris, 1971), remains useful.

only made matters worse, and the night of 24 May witnessed renewed student demonstrations, the most violent of the month. Pompidou meanwhile was continuing his policy of negotiation. On 26–27 May he organized talks between government, unions and employers at the Rue de Grenelle. After hours of negotiations, an agreement was reached thanks to the moderation of the communist CGT. It looked as if the crisis would be resolved, but the workers of the Renault factory repudiated their leaders, and the strikes continued.

The failure of the Grenelle agreement opened the third phase of the crisis: the entry of the politicians. On 28 May, Mitterrand announced his readiness to preside over a provisional government to prepare elections. Not to be outdone, the PCF announced a demonstration for 29 May to take place on the Right Bank – uncomfortably near the Elysée Palace. What did this mean? No one knew, but Pompidou moved tanks into the neighbourhood of Paris.

On 29 May, which already promised to be tense, de Gaulle, silent since 24 May, suddenly disappeared. Ostensibly he had left Paris for Colombey, but instead he paid a mysterious visit to General Massu, commander of French forces in Germany at Baden-Baden. For a few hours de Gaulle's whereabouts were unknown even to his own Prime Minister. Meanwhile, the communist demonstration in Paris passed off peacefully. On 30 May de Gaulle returned, met with his government, and in the afternoon broadcast for a second time (on the radio alone). This time his tone was aggressive: he would not resign, the referendum was to be postponed, parliament dissolved, and elections held. Immediately after this speech, huge crowds poured out into the Champs Elysées to demonstrate support for de Gaulle. The Events of 1968 were over.

The country returned to normal with surprising speed. The elections in June resulted in a Gaullist landslide. In spite of this success, when in April 1969 de Gaulle did finally hold the referendum he had promised in the previous year, he was defeated. Although not constitutionally required to resign, he chose to do so. Less than a year after May 1968, he was no longer President of France.

One striking feature of this narrative is that for a total of fifteen days either de Gaulle or his Prime Minister was absent from France, but this was the result of unfortunate timing not suicidal negligence. Pompidou had left France on 2 May, the day before the first major outbreak of student violence – which no one had predicted. Similarly de Gaulle left on 14 May, just after the peaceful outcome of the previous day's demonstration led to hopes that the situation would return to normal; again, no one had predicted the strikes which followed. May 1968 was certainly full of ironies.

After this brief chronology, I propose to examine four aspects of de Gaulle's role in, and response to, the May crisis. First, what was his responsibility for the escalation of the crisis: could the Events have been avoided if he had acted differently? Secondly, what was behind de Gaulle's mysterious disappearance on 29 May? Thirdly, once the crisis was over, what was de Gaulle's interpretation of it? Finally, what were the effects of May 1968 on the last two years of de Gaulle's life and on the future of Gaullism?

De Gaulle and the escalation of the crisis

After the Events, Alfred Fabre-Luce, a relentless and professional anti-Gaullist since the war, wrote a little book imagining de Gaulle being put on trial by the students in the Sorbonne.[5] This amusing fantasy bears little relation to the truth. In examining de Gaulle's role during the crisis up to 29 May, one immediately comes up against a problem: his invisibility, almost irrelevance, both as protagonist and target of attack. He did figure prominently in the slogans of the 13 May demonstration – 'To the museum with de Gaulle', 'To the archives with de Gaulle' – but this was irresistible since the demonstration coincided with the tenth anniversary of the Algerian *coup* which had brought him to power. Hence the most popular slogan of all: 'Ten years are enough'. But unlike the participants of previous Parisian upheavals the students of 1968 displayed no interest in the symbols of political power: they occupied a university and a theatre. Their ambitions hardly extended outside the Latin Quarter.

There were exceptions to this: for example, the so-called 'long march' of 7 May crossed to the Right Bank and proceeded up the Champs Elysées. On this occasion, the fact that the demonstrators ignored the parliament building, past which they marched, might be interpreted as a tribute to de Gaulle's successful emasculation of parliament – they were children of the Fifth Republic – but their equal lack of interest in the Elysée Palace was symptomatic of a deeper indifference. Christian Fouchet, Minister of the Interior, had received warning of a possible attack on de Gaulle on 8 May, when he was due to mount the Champs Elysées and place a wreath on the tomb of the unknown soldier. In the event nothing happened, not even hostile demonstrations: the students had other matters on their minds.[6] The Gaullist journalist Michel Droit, who watched de Gaulle on the Champs Elysées, remembered his being almost totally alone.[7] Pompidou's closest adviser, Michel Jobert, believed that on 13 May the demonstrators could have taken the Elysée – but no

[5] A. Fabre-Luce, *Le Général en Sorbonne* (Les Brulots, Paris, 1968).
[6] C. Fouchet, *Mémoires d' hier et de demain*, Vol. 1, *Au Service du Général de Gaulle* (Plon, Paris, 1971), p.233.
[7] M. Droit, *Les Feux du crépuscule. Journal, 1968–1969–1970* (Plon, Paris, 1977), pp.21–2.

one thought of doing so.[8] It was this which for de Gaulle made the situation so *insaisissable* (elusive), a word he used frequently at the time.

The absence of de Gaulle from the preoccupations of the generation of 1968 did not signify lingering respect for his legend. The heroic de Gaulle of the war years was for them ancient history, and their attitude to history was cavalier – as was demonstrated by the celebrated chant 'CRS equals SS'.[9] Such sloganistic simplifications shocked many older people otherwise sympathetic to the students, but it demonstrated the extent to which 1968 was a conflict of generations in which the post-war generations contested the authority of those two forces in French politics whose influence derived from the war: the communists and the Gaullists.

The divorce between de Gaulle and the young went back to the mid-1960s. In March 1960 and March 1963 de Gaulle's popularity among 20–35 year olds was almost exactly the same as in the population at large; by 1966 the young were among the most anti-Gaullist sections of the population. It was the over-65s, on the other hand, who were most consistently loyal to de Gaulle.[10] But it is wrong to talk about *the* generation of 1968 since May 1968 was in fact made by two distinct generations, each relating differently to de Gaulle.[11] First there was the generation of the student leaders: Alain Geismar (born 1939), Jacques Sauvageot (b. 1943), Daniel Cohn-Bendit (b.1945); or the Trotskyists Alain Krivine (b.1941) and Henri Weber (b.1944). Sometimes up to ten years older than the mass of students, they were a highly politicized generation marked by the Algerian War, a generation which had looked to the PCF to lead the struggle against that war, and had been disappointed by its failure to do so; a Marxist generation which had discovered its identity in revolt against the PCF; a generation which looked to Che or Mao: in short, a *gauchiste* generation. For such people in 1968, de Gaulle was irrelevant. As Régis Debray (b. 1940) remembers,[12] they were good Marxists who did not analyse politics in terms of personality: they denounced not de

[8] M. Jobert, *Mémoires de l'avenir* (Grasset, Paris, 1974), pp.40–1.

[9] Compagnie Républicaine de Sécurité, the paramilitary police force used in riot control.

[10] In 1960, 67 per cent of those between 20 and 34 declared themselves 'satisfied' with de Gaulle, 22 per cent 'dissatisfied', and 11 per cent had no opinion. In 1963, the respective figures were 45 per cent, 35 per cent and 20 per cent; in 1966, 62 per cent, 29 per cent, 9 per cent. Within the population as a whole the respective figures for 1960 were 69 per cent, 22 per cent, 9 per cent; for 1963, 46 per cent, 36 per cent, 18 per cent; for 1966, 65 per cent, 25 per cent, 10 per cent. See J. Charlot, *Les Français et de Gaulle* (Plon, Paris, 1971), pp.209–11.

[11] D. Berthaux, D. Linhart, D. Le Wita, 'Mai 1968 et la formation des générations politiques en France', *Le Mouvement social*, 173 (1988), pp.75–89. H. Hamon and P. Rotman, *Génération*, Vol. 1, *Les Années de rêve* (Seuil, Paris, 1987), is the fullest account.

[12] R. Debray, *A Demain de Gaulle* (Paris, Gallimard, 1990), p.10. The same point emerges from A. Geismar, S. July, E. Orane, *Vers la guerre civile* (Editions et Publications Premières, Paris, 1969).

Gaulle but a more abstract *pouvoir gaulliste* (Gaullist power), de Gaulle being merely the plaything of capital. The real enemy was the Communist Party whose hold over the working class was the principal obstacle to revolution.

The mass of students belonged not to this generation but, in the words of one contemporary, to 'the depoliticized and routinized cohort of the French who are under twenty years old'.[13] For them, the Fourth Republic was history, the Algerian War an indistinct memory; their experience of politics was the complacent Fifth Republic. This was less a generation that had grown up in opposition to Gaullism, than one that, sentimentally at least, had grown up outside it. Avid consumers of a developing youth culture, they listened to Johnny Hallyday and read *Salut les Copains*; they were, as one writer puts it, the generation of Lennon not Lenin.[14] Nothing shows their relative depoliticization more vividly than the state of the student union, the Union Nationale des Etudiants de France. In the late 1950s it had been at the forefront of the struggle against the Algerian War with a membership of 100,000 in 1962; by 1968 the membership was only 45,000 despite a massive increase in student numbers. Before 1968 the issue which had mobilized these students was not the Vietnam War – the concern of the *gauchistes* – but whether male students could have access to female halls of residence. Many of the most characteristic slogans of 1968 were to be libertarian, sexual, hedonistic or playful: 'pleasure without hindrance'; 'beneath the paving stones the beach'.

If it seems paradoxical to describe the generation which created one of the greatest upheavals in French history as non-political, it could be said instead that while for the *gauchistes* 1968 was, though they did not realize it, the beginning of the end, for the following generation, it demonstrated that the questions which had troubled their adolescence could become the stuff of politics in the future. But this was to be a new political language so far removed from Gaullist discourse as hardly to be able to engage with it. Why take the Elysée if one wants 'the imagination in power', if indeed, as another celebrated slogan had it, 'power is in the street'.

De Gaulle, then, was largely invisible as an object of attack; he was hardly more visible as a protagonist. Until the disastrous 24 May speech, he was remarkable for his silence, remarkable because during the Fifth Republic de Gaulle had ruled France through words – through theatrical press conferences and television monologues. The Fifth Republic had been born from a press conference, the 1961 Algerian *putsch* crushed by a speech. But suddenly in 1968 the words – like 'power' (in the Fifth Republic they were often the same) – were in the street. 1968 was a

[13] François Nourissier, quoted by M. Winock in *Chronique des années soixante* (Seuil, Paris, 1987), p.99.
[14] Joffrin, *Mai 1968*, p.31.

revolution of words which spewed out in endless debates, graffiti, manifestos. De Gaulle, who had turned politics into theatre, was confronted by a movement which quite literally – as in the occupation of the Odeon – turned theatre into politics. Nothing symbolized this inversion better than the night of 10 May when the whole of France – including most ministers – lived a revolution in the making on their radios as reporters described with feverish excitement the construction of the barricades, just as in 1961 French soldiers had huddled around their radios, but on that occasion to listen to de Gaulle denounce the Algerian rebels. In 1968, the radio also was 'in the street' and de Gaulle's only public pronouncement before 24 May was to let his views be known through his ministers after his return from Romania: 'reform yes; chaos [*la chienlit*] no'.

De Gaulle was silent partly because in his view questions of public order – as he viewed the events at first – concerned the government not the head of state, a position which the Prefect of Police, Maurice Grimaud, criticizes in his memoirs.[15] Although some people urged de Gaulle to speak, he believed in the supreme importance of timing, and in this he was supported by Pompidou. While de Gaulle hesitated on 14 May as to whether he should proceed with his scheduled visit to Romania, Pompidou argued that de Gaulle should go; he must not intervene prematurely: 'do not waste yourself'.[16]

Before leaving for Romania de Gaulle had let it be known that he would finally speak on 24 May. One problem with this timing was that the speech occurred in a context different from that for which it had been conceived: de Gaulle had hoped to outline the lessons to be learnt from 1968 once order had returned; instead, as he spoke, the situation was progressively deteriorating. The 24 May broadcast was insufficiently firm for those who wanted a return to order, too vague for the reformers. In contrast to his usually decisive tone in moments of crisis – 'I give the order' (29 January 1960), 'I order ... I forbid' (23 April 1961) – de Gaulle's listeners were treated to some philosophical speculations in which the imperious 'I' was absent. By everyone, friends and enemies alike, the speech was judged to have been an unmitigated disaster. De Gaulle himself supposedly commented: 'I missed the mark'; Pompidou merely remarked to his advisers that 'it could have been worse'.[17]

For the first time in his career, we are told, de Gaulle's words did not work their magic.[18] Although this is not quite true – when the week of the barricades broke out in Algiers in January 1960, de Gaulle's initial

[15] M. Grimaud, *En mai fais ce qu' il te plaît* (Paris, Stock, 1977), p.150. Curiously for a Prefect of Police, Grimaud's sympathies were very much with the students: at one point he even regrets that de Gaulle did not become the Mao of France's 1968.

[16] J.-R. Tournoux, *Le Mois de mai du Général* (Plon, Paris, 1969), p.95.

[17] Balladur, *L' Arbre de mai*, p.24.

[18] P. Alexandre, *L' Elysée en péril* (Livre de poche, Paris, 1971), p.103.

broadcast on 24 January had no effect and it took a second one four days later to bring the rising to an end – at least no previous speech by de Gaulle had actually made things worse. What most people gleaned from de Gaulle's 24 May broadcast was that, once again, he was offering the French people a plebiscite disguised as a referendum. But in his defence it should be noted that at this stage almost no one in the government, Pompidou included, was advocating the parliamentary elections which ultimately proved to be the way out.[19]

De Gaulle in May 1968 was, then, largely absent and silent, but that is not to say that he was without influence. His instincts were consistently for a tough policy: a return to order without concessions. The result, until Pompidou returned, was that government policy was totally incoherent because his ministers were terrified at the prospect of bloodshed on the scale of February 1934 which would have had incalculable political ramifications. During the night of the barricades de Gaulle's ministers left him asleep, for fear of the kind of orders he might give if woken up.

Twice, once before Pompidou returned and once after, de Gaulle intervened with significant consequences. On 8 May, Alain Peyrefitte, Minister of Education, had caused astonishment by announcing that under certain conditions the Sorbonne could be reopened. This was widely misinterpreted by the press as a goverment capitulation and when Sauvageot announced the following day that once the Sorbonne was reopened the students would occupy it, a furious de Gaulle forced Peyrefitte to backtrack. But after Pompidou's return, de Gaulle allowed his Prime Minister a free hand to pursue his conciliatory policy. Given that he remained personally favourable to a tough line, this change of policy is slightly curious.[20] But de Gaulle liked to see his Prime Ministers assuming their responsibilities, and Pompidou, arriving from abroad tanned and energetic, was a welcome change from the ashen-faced exhaustion of de Gaulle's ministers after the night of the barricades.

For those who see the events of 1968 less as some 'crisis of civilization' than as the result of government miscalculations, these two decisions by de Gaulle – disavowing Peyrefitte on 9 May and backing Pompidou on 12 May – were crucial moments. Some argue that it was on 8–9 May that the student movement became radicalized. On the night of 8 May a tearful Geismar, hitherto fairly moderate, appeared at a meeting of Cohn-Bendit's more radical supporters and proclaimed a startling *mea culpa* which reflected the students' frustration at how little they had

[19] When this plan was proposed to the Council of Ministers on 23 May, only three ministers – Gorse, Missoffe and Guichard – preferred elections. See O. Guichard, *Mon Général* (Grasset, Paris, 1980), p.426.
[20] On 19 May he demanded the forcible evacuation of the Sorbonne and Odéon, to the horror of Grimaud, Fouchet and Pompidou, and only at the last moment did Pompidou succeed in getting this operation called off.

achieved. If, it is argued, the government had offered concessions on 8 May when the attitude of some student leaders hung in the balance, the discontent might have fizzled out. This may or may not be true, but de Gaulle's vetoing of Peyrefitte's compromise cannot have been the decisive factor since it occurred after – to some extent in response to – Geismar's 'conversion' and Sauvageot's inflammatory comments about occupying the Sorbonne. The problem at this stage was that Pompidou's absence prevented any consistent policy.

The decision to reopen the Sorbonne on 11 May is seen by most observers as the turning point of the events. Pompidou's defenders argue that had the Sorbonne not been reopened, the demonstration of 13 May would have led to an assault on the building. As it was, the day passed off without incident: why storm a citadel which had already been surrendered? Pompidou believed he had possibly averted a civil war. The alternative view, shared by Raymond Aron and by Peyrefitte, who resigned in disgust, is that the government's capitulation on 11 May was the cause of the strikes which started three days later.[21] In the words of Fouchet, reopening the Sorbonne caused the government to 'lose the war when it had not even lost the battle'.[22] De Gaulle came to the same view: 'it was worthy of Pétain, not de Gaulle' *(ce n'était pas du de Gaulle, c'etait du Pétain).*[23]

It is certainly true that Pompidou had misjudged the situation. 'It'll be over in forty-eight hours' he reassured de Gaulle who was about to leave for Romania: forty-eight hours later the country was moving towards paralysis. But it is less often remembered that Pompidou's strategy was partially successsful. Although in the collective memory May 1968 lives as a month of violence and barricades, there were only six days of violence which occurred in two separate phases. The first took place on 3, 6 and 10 May. As Pompidou had hoped, the reopening of the Sorbonne led to a period of calm broken only when the government forbade Cohn-Bendit, who was a German citizen, to re-enter France: this led to three further nights of rioting between 22 and 24 May. On this last day the violence took on a semi-insurrectionary character, and opinion became hostile to the students. But the consequences of bloodshed in the earlier part of the month, while the students were still popular, might well have proved fatal to the regime; Pompidou prevented such an outcome. The students were more harmless in the Sorbonne than in the street. In short, de Gaulle's influence in 1968, such as it was, only aggravated the situation, and to the extent that he regretted his backing

[21] R. Aron, *La Révolution introuvable* (Fayard, Paris, 1968), pp.42–3; A. Peyrefitte, in *France Soir*, 25 May 1978.

[22] C. Fouchet, *Mémoires d' hier et de demain*, Vol. 2, *Les Lauriers sont coupés* (Plon, Paris, 1973), p.41.

[23] Fouchet, *Les Lauriers*, p.44.

for Pompidou's conciliatory policy, he was almost certainly wrong. In May 1968 de Gaulle's touch had certainly deserted him.

De Gaulle's disappearance: 29 May

Between 24 and 29 May, de Gaulle seemed to have become not just irrelevant but almost entirely forgotten. The names on all lips were those of Mitterrand and Mendès France; the question in all minds was: what did the PCF intend to do? Then suddenly de Gaulle's spectacular initiative on 29 May transformed the situation.

Apart from this bald account, 29 May remains one of the more mysterious moments of de Gaulle's career. This is not because we lack information about what happened. The major protagonists have all provided their own versions which coincide on all but the tiniest details of *la petite histoire:* when Massu was awoken from his afternoon siesta to hear that de Gaulle would be arriving imminently was he 'starkers' (*à poil*), as one witness believes, or was he wearing a red polo neck jumper and corduroys? Despite such nuggets of controversy, the essential chronology is well-established.[24]

On 28 May de Gaulle received in succession at the Elysée, the agricultural trade unionist Michel Debatisse (4 p.m.), Michel Droit (7 p.m.), Pompidou and Fouchet. They all found his mood apocalyptic: Droit was told that the French had never got over the defeats of Sedan and Waterloo. But there were also signs that de Gaulle was hatching something. To Debatisse de Gaulle revealed that he planned to speak. Droit was there ostensibly to discuss a possible television interview in which de Gaulle might remedy the effects of his 24 May broadcast. He was ushered out by a side door so that Pompidou, who had just arrived, would not see him. And none of these visitors knew that earlier in the day de Gaulle had phoned his son-in-law, Alain de Boissieu, summoning him for the next morning, or that Mme de Gaulle had phoned up her brother, Jacques Vendroux, asking him if on the next day he could take the General's maid Jeanne home to her village: she was being given a 'few days' holiday for reasons that could not yet be revealed.[25]

[24] The most thorough sifting of the evidence is by F. Goguel, 'Charles de Gaulle du 24 mai au 28 mai 1968', *Espoir*, 46 (1984), pp.3–14, and, more recently, J. Lacouture, *De Gaulle*, Vol. 2, *The Leader*, (1986; English translation: Collins-Harvill, London, 1991). The most important accounts by those involved directly in the events of that day are: A. de Boissieu, *Pour servir le Général* (Plon, Paris, 1983), pp.175–94; J. Massu, *Baden 68: souvenirs d' une fidélité gaulliste* (Plon, Paris, 1979), pp.175–84; F. Flohic, *Souvenirs d' outre-Gaulle* (Plon, Paris, 1979), pp.172–84. Information on 28 May is contained in Droit, *Les Feux du crépuscule*, pp.33–42; and Fouchet, *Les Lauriers*, pp.19–27. It is Flohic who remembers Massu telling him that he was 'à poil'. Unless otherwise stated my account comes from the above sources.

[25] J. Vendroux, *Ces Grandes années que j' ai vécues*, Vol. 2, *1958–70* (Plon, Paris, 1975), p.318.

When Vendroux picked up Jeanne the following day, she told him that the de Gaulles had left the Elysée that morning with more luggage than they usually took for Colombey. De Gaulle had already had a busy morning. At 9 a.m. Matignon was informed that the Council of Ministers scheduled for that afternoon was to be postponed until the following day. At 10.15 a.m. Boissieu arrived. He found his father-in-law depressed and arguing that he might as well retire to write his memoirs. Boissieu assured him of army loyalty, and de Gaulle thereupon announced he would sound out the views of General Massu. Then he would speak to the nation from Colombey, Strasbourg or elswhere. Possibly he would spend the night at Mulhouse where Boissieu was stationed. Meanwhile Boissieu was instructed to contact Massu and arrange a meeting with de Gaulle at Sainte-Odile in Alsace, or at Strasbourg. Should this prove impossible to organize, de Gaulle would himself go to Baden.

At 11 a.m. de Gaulle rang Pompidou and told him that he needed a day to reflect at Colombey. But de Gaulle's words only alarmed Pompidou further: 'I am old, you are young, the future is yours. Farewell, I embrace you'. This, especially the unusual intimacy of the final phrase – 'it wasn't his style', said Pompidou – sounded more like *adieu* than *au revoir*. As Jacques Chaban-Delmas put it: 'He embraces you and it's you who are screwed' (*Il vous embrasse et c'est vous qui êtes baisé*). Immediately after this conversation, the presidential couple, accompanied by de Gaulle's aide, Admiral Flohic, left the Elysée for the heliport of Issy les Moulineaux. Loading the helicopter took longer than usual because of the extra luggage. At 1 p.m. they landed at St. Dizier to refuel. Here de Gaulle expected a message from Boissieu about the rendezvous with Massu, but Boissieu had been unable to reach Baden. De Gaulle therefore set off himself for Germany.

On arrival at Baden, de Gaulle's first words to Massu were 'it's all up' (*tout est foutu*). While the two men talked in Massu's study, Mme Massu looked after Mme de Gaulle and had bedrooms prepared for the unexpected visitors. De Gaulle poured out his bile to Massu, and asked that the Federal government be informed of his presence in Germany. Massu tried to boost his morale. At the end of their private conversation de Gaulle was suddenly resolute again: he would leave for Colombey at once. By 6.30 p.m. the de Gaulles and Flohic were back at Colombey. That evening de Gaulle was cheerful enough to quote some of his own poetry to Flohic. By midday on 30 May he was back in Paris where he chaired the Council of Ministers at 3 p.m. At 4.30 p.m. he delivered his four-minute radio speech. This time it was clear that the party was over, a fact underlined by the massive Gaullist demonstration which followed it.

How are these events to be interpreted? Massu and Pompidou believe de Gaulle had lost his nerve. He went to Baden intending to take refuge abroad until Massu's eloquence restored his confidence. Flohic and de

Boissieu, on the other hand, argue that de Gaulle the master tactician had cold-bloodedly stage-managed a psychological *coup* which allowed him to regain the political initiative. These different interpretations are not entirely dispassionate. For Flohic and Boissieu, de Gaulle could do no wrong, while Massu, who had quarrelled with de Gaulle over Algeria, was not unhappy to paint himself such a glorious role. As for Pompidou, he was deeply resentful of having received such 'cavalier treatment' *(singulière désinvolture)*, as he puts it, but he did not actually see de Gaulle on 29 May, and his version of events is based on what Massu told him. The most detailed analysis, by the historian François Goguel, concludes that while de Gaulle had been tempted a few days earlier to give up, by 29 May that temptation had been overcome. His plan on 29 May was to create a political *coup de théâtre*: 29 May was a day of decision following the days of despair. Jean Lacouture, however, believes that de Gaulle's mood on 29 May was still extremely volatile: he had left Paris firmly determined to carry on, but by the time he reached Baden, after an exhausting helicopter journey, particularly testing for a man of seventy-eight who had hardly slept for several nights, his resolve had weakened and he had again been temporarily tempted to give up.

As for de Gaulle himself, he admitted several times that he had come near to giving up.[26] He told Flohic on the evening of 29 May that if he had not come back he would have stayed a while in Germany, then Ireland, then 'much further away'. On another occasion, he compared his mood to various other moments in his career – September 1940, March 1942, January 1946, 1954, December 1965 – when he had given up the struggle or been tempted to do so. This grand historical fresco must be treated with a pinch of salt since the myth of the man of destiny, sacrificing domestic tranquility for the call of history, was the stock-in-trade of de Gaulle's personal mythology. None the less, there seems little doubt that after the débâcle of 24 May, de Gaulle's nerve did fail and that he had been tempted to give up; and indeed it would have been amazing had he not been. The problem is whether by 29 May he had overcome the temptation or whether it was on 29 May that he finally did so.

The question can best be approached by examining first de Gaulle's mood and then his intentions. De Gaulle's temperament was, as many writers observe, cyclomythic. He went through periodic bouts of melancholy which fed into his natural propensity for deep philosophical pessimism: Nietzsche's 'nothing is worth anything' *(rien ne vaut rien)* was a favourite phrase. After 24 May he was certainly cast into such a mood

---

[26] For example, to Bernard Tricot: see G. Pilleul, *L' Entourage et de Gaulle*, (Plon, Paris, 1979), p.319; to Pierre Lefranc: see P. Lefranc, *Avec qui vous savez* (Plon, Paris, 1979), p.280; to Michel Droit: see C. de Gaulle, *Discours et messages*, Vol. 5, *Vers le terme* (Livre de Poche, Paris, 1970), p.322.

and all his interlocutors on 28 and 29 May were subjected to a tirade of gloom. But de Gaulle was also prone to paint the blackest possible picture of events in order to shock his listener into a reaction. This was a tactic familiar to those who knew de Gaulle well, and they had a phrase to describe it. Thus on 28 May when Michel Droit, no intimate of de Gaulle's, confided his worries about the general to André Dewavrin, who had known de Gaulle since 1940, he was told that the general was probably playing the *coup de l'apocalypse*.

There is reason to believe that 28–29 May was one of those moments when the apocalyptic predictions must not be taken at face value. We know from de Gaulle's comments to Droit and Debatisse on 28 May that he intended to speak publicly again and his departure on the next day was planned with a meticulous secrecy that does not suggest a man at the end of his tether. One account points out, apropos of the 'I embrace you' which so alarmed Pompidou, that, although rare on de Gaulle's lips, this phrase was invariably used by him on the eve of decisive moments of action, for example to Leclerc just before the Liberation of Paris.[27] In short, if de Gaulle's words were a torrent of despair, his actions were calculated, and Massu, who had never been close to him and was not known for psychological subtlety – 'Massu was Massu' de Gaulle told Boissieu – was taken in.

It follows from this – to move from mood to intentions – that de Gaulle had not gone to Baden in despair to seek refuge abroad. Indeed his original plan had been to meet Massu in France. His instruction to inform the German government of his presence was a diplomatic courtesy not necessarily implying a long stay. As for the substantial luggage, it proved only that de Gaulle had considered the possibility of a few days away from Paris – as the 'holiday' for Jeanne shows – and it was only Mme Massu – her short testimony, reported by her husband, in fact contains a significant error – who started to make up beds on the assumption that de Gaulle was staying in Germany.[28] His original intention, we have seen, was to follow his meeting with Massu by a speech to the nation, possibly from Strasbourg, possibly from Colombey.

But why leave Paris at all? One possible reason was to ensure that if the communist demonstration of 29 May did have ulterior motives, the Elysée would not be a target: 'one doesn't attack an empty palace'. The idea of leaving Paris to regain freedom of manœuvre was tactically characteristic of de Gaulle, always an advocate of movement over immobility. During barricades week in Algiers in January 1960 de Gaulle had counselled his representative, Delouvrier, to withdraw from the city of

---

[27] A. and P. Rouanet, *Les Trois derniers chagrins du Général de Gaulle* (Grasset et Fasquelle, Paris, 1980), pp.302–4.
[28] She reports that Mme de Gaulle had told her that the de Gaulles had stopped at Colombey before arriving in Baden (Massu, *Baden 68*, p.82).

Algiers; during the 1961 *putsch* he had himself contemplated leaving Paris. Earlier during the Events of 1968 his son had advised him to leave Paris for, say, Brest; and Fouchet had recommended Thiers's ignored advice to Louis Philippe in 1848: a move to Versailles.

The mysterious departure from Paris on 29 May did not therefore come out of nowhere. Its fundamental purpose was to create a political shock at the very moment when the entry into the fray of the politicians made the situation no longer *insaisissable*. It was time to move in for the kill. All this was entirely consistent with de Gaulle's whole philosophy of political action as outlined in his 1932 *The Edge of the Sword* – a philosophy based around ruse, contemplation, silence, surprise, and then action.

One can finally ask if such drama was really necessary, or, if it was, whether in itself it would have sufficed to resolve the situation. Pompidou had come to the view that parliamentary elections were necessary: these would not be open to the plebiscitary accusations levelled against the referendum, and with the students increasingly unpopular, the government would certainly win them. But when de Gaulle returned to Paris on 30 May he had drafted a speech which ruled out both referendum and dissolution. It was Pompidou who insisted on a dissolution, threatening resignation if he did not get his way. At the last minute de Gaulle conceded. Without the tense atmosphere created by de Gaulle's disappearance, would the announcement of a dissolution have been enough? Without offering the *dénouement* of a dissolution, would de Gaulle's speech have done the trick? Jean Charlot convincingly argues that Pompidou and de Gaulle deserve equal credit.[29] Finally we must not forget the demonstration which followed de Gaulle's speech. This had been planned for several days by a number of Gaullists, most notably Pierre Lefranc.[30] The go-ahead for a demonstration on 30 May had been given unenthusiastically by Pompidou on 28 May, but no one had predicted that the demonstration would take place in such propitious circumstances. De Gaulle would normally have spoken at 8 p.m. but it was pointed out by his adviser Jacques Foccart that since a demonstration had been planned for 5 p.m. he should speak before it. Thus de Gaulle spoke at 4.30 p.m. The demonstration provided instantaneous evidence of the impact which de Gaulle's words had had. The organizers of the demonstration had also played their part in de Gaulle's triumph.

---

[29] J. Charlot, 'The Aftermath of May 68 for Gaullism' in D. Hanley and A. Kerr, *May 68. Coming of Age* (Macmillan, London, 1989), p.65. On the taking of the decision for the referendum, see Bernard Tricot's contribution in Pilleul, *L'Entourage*, p.318–23.
[30] Lefranc, *Avec qui vous savez*, pp.267–81.

De Gaulle's interpretation of 1968

After the elections of June 1968 de Gaulle is said to have commented: 'It's a PSF parliament which I'll make carry out a PSU policy' (*voilà une chambre PSF à qui je ferai faire une politique PSU*).[31] The remark may be apocryphal but it neatly encapsulates the truth that once the events were over, de Gaulle's interpretation of them was far from generally shared by his own supporters, many of whom accepted the view of the new Minister of the Interior, Raymond Marcellin, that May 1968 had been a conspiracy master-minded from Havana.

De Gaulle offered two interpretations of the events – one contained in embryo in his speech of 24 May and the other in his speech of 30 May. As the second speech described it, nihilistic 'agitators' had tried to drag France back into the 'abyss' from which de Gaulle had already rescued her twice. This situation was then exploited by the Communist Party which sighted an opportunity to seize power.

Attacking the communists was a classic way of rallying conservative support, but de Gaulle himself knew that his allegations bore little relation to reality. Indeed during the Grenelle negotiations the communist CGT had been infintely more accommodating than the other trade unions; and earlier in the month two Gaullist deputies, Jean de Lipkowski and de Gaulle's own brother-in-law, Vendroux, had been approached by leading communists privately offering the party's support to de Gaulle.[32] On the other hand many people, including Pompidou, believed that the party's announcement of a demonstration on 29 May signified a change in policy. Grimaud was warned on that day, by officials acting for both Fouchet and Pompidou, to guard against an attack on the Hôtel de Ville. So in these last, tense days of May, when Paris was thick with rumour, de Gaulle may have genuinely anticipated a communist move.

De Gaulle's less polemical interpretation of 1968 was sketched out in his 24 May broadcast and much elaborated upon thereafter. In this view, the events mirrored the 'alienation' caused by a 'modern mechanical civilization' where individuals scurried about like ants, lacking control over their lives – whether in the factory, the universities or the regions. The remedy was to be a 'new contact and co-operation between rulers and ruled'. This was the alleged purpose of the 1969 referendum.

---

[31] F. Bon, 'Le Référendum du 27 avril: suicide politique ou nécessité stratégique', *Revue française de science politique,* 20/2 (1970), p.209. The PSF (Parti Social Français) was the name adopted in 1936 by the most well-known of the 1930s right wing extra-parliamentary leagues. The PSU (Parti Socialiste Unifié), was a small but coherent and influential party on the left, a kind of *gauchiste* intellectual power-house in the 1960s. Thus de Gaulle meant to suggest that he was going to try and impose a reforming programme on a very right-wing parliament.

[32] Alexandre, *L' Elysée en péril,* p.278; Vendroux, *Ces Grandes Années,* pp.316–17.

140 *De Gaulle and Twentieth-Century France*

As early as 1941 in a speech at Oxford, de Gaulle had criticized the way in which the uniformity of modern civilization crushed individualism. During the RPF period he had advocated an 'association' between capital and labour – a middle way between oppressive communism and alienating capitalism. In the first years of the Fifth Republic de Gaulle seemed to have shelved these ideas and up to 1965 he made almost no reference to either 'participation' or 'association'.[33] But from 1965 onwards he returned to the theme regularly, although efforts to translate it into legislation were thwarted by Pompidou's lack of enthusiasm and by uncertainty as to how to do so anyway. De Gaulle none the less continued to harp on the notion, and in March 1968 he also broached the idea of the need for decentralization. These ideas were very much in the tradition of social Catholicism which had been strong in the Nord region from which de Gaulle's family originated; they also possibly owed something to the so-called 'noncomformists of the 1930s' with whom he had had many contacts.[34] But this takes us far from the world of 1968: what validity did de Gaulle's views have as an interpretation of the Events of that year?

Although there have been innumerable explanations of 1968 – from the contemporary *gauchiste* belief that they were France's 1905 revolution to the more recent suggestion that they were the origin of the materialistic individualism of the 1980s with the generation of 1968 as the ancestors of today's yuppies – the most convincing one is that of Stanley Hoffmann and Michel Crozier who see 1968 as a characteristic example of the French style of protest – the mirror image of an equally French style of authority which refuses compromise and discussion. 1968 was a revolt against what they have labelled the 'blocked society'.[35] In the 1960s this structural problem was exacerbated by the fact that while the country was undergoing a massive economic transformation and a new generation was growing up in a world of democratizing consumerism and material abundance, social institutions – family, school, university – remained strongly imprinted by the cultural values of a rural and provincial France which was being rapidly left behind.

[33] See the statistical analysis of de Gaulle's speeches in J. M. Cotteret and R. Moreau, *Recherches sur le vocabulaire du Général de Gaulle* (Armand Colin, Paris, 1969).
[34] See P. Sigoda, 'Charles de Gaulle, la révolution conservatrice et le personnalisme du mouvement "l' ordre nouveau"', *Espoir*, 46 (1984); J. Barnoud, 'Les Sources de la pensée sociale du Général de Gaulle 1870–1914', *Etudes gaulliennes*, 7/8 (July–November 1974), pp.85–96.
[35] H. Weber, *Vingt ans après* (Seuil, Paris, 1988), gives an excellent survey of interpretations. J. Capdeville and R. Mouriaux, *Mai 68: l'entre-deux de la modernité* (Fondation Nationale des Sciences Politiques, Paris, 1988), does so as well, but overall is a bit disappointing. For the interpretations mentioned in the text, see D. Bensaid and H. Weber, *Mai 68: une répétition générale* (Maspero, Paris, 1968); G. Lipovetsky, *L' Ere du vide* (Gallimard, Paris, 1983); M. Crozier, *The Stalled Society* (1970; English translation: Viking Press, New York, 1973); S. Hoffmann, *Decline or Renewal? France since the 1930s* (Viking, New York, 1974).

If this view is correct, de Gaulle's interpretation of the Events – that they demonstrated the desire for 'a new contact and co-operation between rulers and ruled' – is certainly more interesting than the knee-jerk reaction of most conservatives. But what de Gaulle did not seem to realize – certainly his analysis contains no sense of his responsibility – was that it was Gaullism which reinforced those features of French society which sociologists like Crozier have excoriated. De Gaulle was himself the supreme embodiment of precisely everything that 1968 was against. His press conferences were artfully staged exercises in showmanship. The crowd-baths of his provincial tours were plunges into anonymous crowds, not attempts to engage with the problems of individual Frenchmen, all the more so since his severe short-sightedness meant that he could quite literally not distinguish faces: the crowds were a blur and that is how he liked them. Elections were regularly presented as a choice between de Gaulle or anarchy, and intermediary institutions were treated with contempt. In short, de Gaulle's Republic did not train its electors in citizenship and responsibliity; it treated them as minors. And 1968 was the revolt of the children against their fathers. De Gaulle failed to acknowledge that in 1968 that he was an integral part of the problem that he diagnosed.

The aftermath of 1968

'You know, he has suffered so much for two years.' Mme de Gaulle spoke these words on the evening of de Gaulle's death on 9 November 1970. Why two years? Presumably because 1968 was an experience from which de Gaulle never recovered. Pierre-Louis Blanc, a former Elysée press officer who, as an assistant in the drafting of de Gaulle's memoirs saw more of him than did most people in the last year of his life, speaks of 'this open wound which remained present in him until his death'.[36] What was the nature of this suffering, this wound, and why did it occur when, after all, de Gaulle had emerged triumphant from the Events?

The most immediate consequence of May 1968 was the breach with Pompidou. During most of the crisis, while de Gaulle floundered, it was the indefatigable Pompidou who kept the government afloat. Fouchet, Debré, Peyrefitte, all ministers whose primary loyalty was to de Gaulle, were brushed aside by Pompidou's team of young protégés – Balladur, Jobert, Jacques Chirac. Peyrefitte had been disavowed in Pompidou's reopening of the Sorbonne. Debré, whose portfolio ought to have involved him in the Grenelle negotiations, was entirely ignored by Pompidou who conducted the affair personally with help from Chirac: 'spare me the squawkings of Debré' said Pompidou to de Gaulle. The very fact he could

[36] Blanc, *De Gaulle*, p.48.

talk so disrespectfully revealed how much things had changed in a few weeks. During this hectic period, Pompidou's team developed enduring loyalties to their patron, and a shared sense of *esprit de corps*. As Balladur puts it: 'up to then I had only felt admiration for him; now there was something deeper, born during these days and nights that we few lived at his side'.[37] A Pompidou clan was born.

But, as we have seen, de Gaulle came retrospectively to believe that Pompidou had mishandled the crisis; and Pompidou never forgave de Gaulle for having left him in the lurch on 29 May. Later that year at a private dinner party given by Mauriac, Pompidou's bitterness poured out in a long diatribe. He spoke of the 'appalling hours' he had lived on 29 May; de Gaulle's behaviour, he repeated several times, had been 'inadmissible'; as for Pompidou's wife, she said of de Gaulle, 'I will never forgive him'.[38] A similar bitterness emerges from Pompidou's posthumously published account of May 1968: 'It was I who during the May days negotiated, talked to the country, to the Assembly, to the unions, to the politicians. In the eyes of the masses it was I who held out; General de Gaulle had been "absent"'.[39] Although several other factors contributed to estrange the two men further, the emotional rupture went back to May. When the referendum was announced, Pompidou refused, despite the urging of some Gaullists, to declare that if de Gaulle were defeated he would not stand in any ensuing presidential election. He was quite willing to present himself as an alternative to de Gaulle, and in the process he scotched any possible victory that de Gaulle might have had. Out of May 1968, then, a rival Pompidolian Gaullism was born.

Pompidolianism was not only a competing nexus of allegiances, it was also a distinct, more conservative, interpretation of May 1968. Pompidou liked to think of himself as in touch with the latest cultural trends – he had admired Godard's *La Chinoise*, seeing it as a chilling anticipation of 1968, and he even *tutoyed* Brigitte Bardot – but despite this (or because of it), Pompidou's interpretation of 1968 was more pessimistic than de Gaulle's, even if during the daily management of the crisis de Gaulle had taxed him with being too optimistic.[40] He saw 1968 as a 'crisis of civilization' caused by a younger generation no longer constrained by the traditional disciplines of religion and family.[41] De Gaulle's idea that the malaise that had given birth to the crisis could be remedied by reforms was unrealistic because the students wanted not to participate in society but to destroy it. 'In order to change society, the people who compose it

[37] Balladur, *L' Arbre de mai*, p.359.
[38] C. Mauriac, *Les Espaces imaginaires* (Grasset, Paris, 1975), pp.259–74.
[39] G. Pompidou, *Pour rétablir une vérité* (Flammarion, Paris, 1982), p.199.
[40] Mauriac, *Les Espaces imaginaires*, p.261.
[41] For Pompidou's view of the Events, see G. Pompidou, *Le Noeud gordien* (Plon, Paris, 1975).

have to be changed', he told Michel Droit, tapping his forehead to indicate the folly of de Gaulle's obsession with participation.[42]

In short, if de Gaulle's attitude in 1968 was summed up as 'reform yes, chaos no', Pompidou's was rather, 'chaos yes – because for the moment we have no choice; reform no – because no reform would satisfy the protesters'. After the Events were over, de Gaulle supported the education reforms of Edgar Faure in the face of much hostility from many newly elected Gaullist deputies, but Pompidou, once he had become President, was to be extremely lukewarm about the reforming efforts of his Prime Minister, Chaban-Delmas, whose vision of a 'new society' was partially inspired by the views of such as Crozier. By this time, left-wing Gaullists like Louis Vallon viewed Pompidou as *l'anti-de Gaulle.*

The year 1968 allowed Pompidou to emerge as a major political figure in his own right, and to forge his own relationship with the electorate. To some extent this was bound to be at the expense of de Gaulle, but it is wrong to see May 1968 as creating some irreversible breach between de Gaulle and the French people. In fact, it is remarkable how little effect May 1968 had on de Gaulle's popularity. The lowest point of popularity of his presidency was reached not in 1968 but in 1963 during the miners' strike. This was the only year when the proportion of those declaring themselves 'satisfied' with de Gaulle fell below 50 per cent. Between May 1968 and April 1969 it fluctuated between 52 per cent and 58 per cent, not so very different from many other years (1964: 50–56 per cent; 1965: 52–61 per cent). Even de Gaulle's defeat in the 1969 referendum did not imply that he had suddenly been repudiated by an electorate shaken by his weakness in 1968. The percentage of those voting *oui* in 1969 was in fact higher than de Gaulle's first ballot score in the 1965 presidential election which could be taken as his level of popularity in normal conditions. The high score of the earlier referenda can be attributed to the peculiar circumstances of the Algerian War.[43]

Nevertheless, 1968 was not without consequences for de Gaulle's relationship with the French people, and for the future of Gaullism. De Gaulle had always aspired to bridge the divide between left and right, to attract support from all quarters. In this he had been not altogether unsuccessful. Although in the 1965 presidential election he did well among traditional conservative voters, such as women and the old, he also attracted significant support from the industrial working class, winning 42 per cent of their votes, better indeed than he did among the professions (41 per cent) or the peasantry (37 per cent). The future success of Gaullism would depend on whether the Gaullist party could permanently capture some of de Gaulle's own personal following. Already

---

[42] Droit, *Les Feux du crépuscule*, p.56.
[43] All figures from Charlot, *Les Français*, pp.209–12.

there were signs in the mid-1960s that this was not happening. In the 1967 parliamentary elections, the Gaullists' support was socially narrower than de Gaulle's: more successful among the professions and business (45 per cent), less so among the workers (30 per cent).[44]

What effect did 1968 have on this pattern? The Gaullist landslide of June 1968 was achieved with an electorate which deviated even more significantly from the social composition of de Gaulle's own electorate. Given the extent to which these elections were a backlash against May 1968 this is not too surprising. But this pattern was sustained in the referendum of 1969 when de Gaulle's own support fell more among those categories in which he had previously been more successful than the Gaullists (a 7 per cent drop among the workers) and less among those where the Gaullists had done traditionally better than he (a 2 per cent drop among the peasants). In other words, his electorate came to resemble more closely the more conservative electorate of the Gaullist parties. The year 1968 started a breach with the workers which had not healed a year later. This tendency was accentuated in the presidential election of 1969 which Pompidou won with an electorate which departed even more from de Gaulle's inter-class support. 1968, the heyday of Gaullism as an electoral force, was also the beginning of its decline.

De Gaulle may not have followed all this psephological detail but he was aware of these trends to the extent that he realized that the parliamentary victory of June 1968 was a conservative backlash not a personal vote of confidence. This was why he called the referendum of 1969. André Malraux claimed afterwards that de Gaulle had designed the referendum as an elegant means of leaving power. But this is almost certainly untrue because when de Gaulle announced it on 2 February there was no reason to think that he would lose. De Gaulle called the referendum partly because he believed in the reforms that he was proposing – although they bore a pretty tangential relationship to 'participation' – but the more fundamental reason was quite simply, as he told Fouchet, that he wanted to 'feel that the nation was with me'.[45] Malraux claims that when he asked de Gaulle why he had chosen to stake his future on such trivial issues, he had replied 'for the absurdity of it'.[46] The remark may be apocryphal but it expressed the truth that for de Gaulle the purpose of the affair was to renew his own personal contract with the people.

The first opinion polls were indeed quite favourable to de Gaulle, but quickly the electorate's mood changed and it became clear that de Gaulle

[44] See J. Charlot, *The Gaullist Phenomenon: the Gaullist Movement in the Fifth Republic* (1970; English translation: Allen and Unwin, London, 1971).
[45] Fouchet, *Les Lauriers*, p.48.
[46] A. Malraux, *Fallen Oaks. Conversation with de Gaulle* (1971; English translation: Hamish Hamilton, London, 1972), p.8.

would lose. At this point, after toying fleetingly with the idea of a tactical retreat, he came to the conclusion that the referendum could after all offer a dignified exit from power. One visitor was told: 'I will be more to France than if I had left for the banal reason that my period of office had expired'.[47] He was haunted by the ravages old age could cause. 'Old age is a shipwreck' he had written of Pétain; and he had been saddened by the last years of Churchill. He had also been shocked by the sudden death in 1959 of his brother Pierre. 'If God grants me life' was a phrase often used by de Gaulle in his last years: death haunted him as well.

Once it became clear he would lose, de Gaulle could hardly wait to go: his main priority was now to complete his memoirs. Another three years in the Elysee, he said, could not equal what he would be able to achieve in his memoirs.[48] This was not merely a rationalization of failure or self-reassurance. Politicians usually write memoirs to justify themselves or alleviate the boredom of retirement, or for money. But de Gaulle's memoirs were to be a way of creating himself as a legend, a mythic icon to become part of the texture of France's history and provide for future generations a vision of what *grandeur* could be, even if for the moment 'mediocrity' prevailed.

De Gaulle's private conversation in the last eighteen months of his life was full of gloomy prognostication and bitter detachment. He had talked in much the same way during the Fourth Republic but at that time he had had hopes of returning to power. This time he had nothing left but to work at his myth. It is astonishing the extent to which his every action in retirement continued to be calculated to the last detail. Apart from a formal telegram of congratulation to Pompidou after his election as President, he made no further public statements; he retired to Colombey and never again did he visit Paris, apart from one incognito appearance at the christening of his granddaughter.[49] Equally he determined to be absent from France on the anniversary of 18 June so that others could not use his glory for their purposes: in June 1969 he went to Ireland, in 1970 to Spain, and in 1971 he had planned to go to China. Otherwise he worked unremittingly on his memoirs and when the first volume was published in 1970 it appeared dramatically in the bookshops without any advance warning. A few days later he was dead.

In silent retirement, then, de Gaulle watched vigilantly over his legend. The year of 1968 had seen the opening of a breach between de Gaulle and the French, a breach which the referendum of 1969 confirmed. De Gaulle therefore sought refuge in the future, in history. As he remarked to an aide on the eve of his defeat: 'the French no longer want de Gaulle.

[47] Droit, *Les Feux du crépuscule*, p.127.
[48] Droit, *Les Feux du crépuscule*, p.196.
[49] Blanc, *De Gaulle*, pp.61–2.

But the myth, you will see the growth of the myth ... in thirty years'.[50]

Little more than twenty years have passed but de Gaulle's prediction seems already to have been vindicated. To an extraordinary degree he has already become part of the national patrimony, one of those *lieux de mémoire* of which Pierre Nora has written – those common points of reference in which a nation recognizes itself. And this is no less true of the ex-*gauchistes* than of anyone else. Thus Roland Castro (b. 1940), one of the first to visit revolutionary Cuba in 1961, a Maoist in 1968, today declares himself 'subjugated' by de Gaulle, finding his 1941 Oxford speech 'one of the finest texts against Nazism ever written'.[51] Serge July (b. 1942), an ally of Geismar in 1968, wrote in *Libération* on 18 June 1990: 'Nowadays, one no longer discusses de Gaulle, one contemplates his legend like a lost continent, that is, when one isn't dreaming of it'. But most striking of all is the recantation of Régis Debray, who spent 1968 in a Bolivian prison after his capture while fighting with Che Guevara. For Debray today 'De Gaulle fills me with happiness. How comforting it is to imagine that he was alive, in our midst. His name will serve for a long time as eraser of mediocrity'. And he finds de Gaulle to be the first great man of the twenty-first century while Mitterrand is the last of the nineteenth century.[52] The cynical might observe that the moment Debray takes up a cause its stock is likely to decline. But for the moment at least, de Gaulle's prestige seems assured. As early as 1971 Claude Mauriac commented to Malraux that it was amongst the former anti-Gaullists and ex-*gauchistes* that de Gaulle's greatness was being most widely recognized. As Malraux replied: 'it wasn't the royalists, but the republicans, who created Jeanne d'Arc'.[53]

If, as we observed at the beginning, for de Gaulle 1968 had been a year of ironies, of ironic discomfitures, perhaps in the end the greatest irony of the story lies altogether elsewhere: in de Gaulle's posthumous triumph by the year of his centenary over those who challenged his authority so dramatically twenty-two years earlier.

[50] Quoted by Lacouture, *The Ruler*, p.574.
[51] *Libération*, 18 June 1990.
[52] Debray, *A Demain de Gaulle*, p.68.
[53] C. Mauriac, *Et comme l' espérance est violente* (Grasset, Paris, 1976).

Select Bibliography

Works by Charles de Gaulle

Le Fil de l'épée (1932); English translation, *The Edge of the Sword* (Faber, London, 1960).

Vers l' armée de métier (1934); English translation, *The Army of the Future* (Hutchinson, London, 1940).

La France et son armée (1938); English translation, *France and her Army* (Hutchinson, London, 1945).

Mémoires de guerre (1954–9, 3 vols.); English translation, *War Memoirs* (Weidenfeld and Nicolson, London, 1955–60); Vol. 1 *The Call to Honour, 1940–1942* (1955); Vol. 2 *Unity, 1942–1944* (1959); Vol. 3 *Salvation 1944–1946* (1960).

Mémoires d' espoir (1970–1, 2 vols.); English translation (in one volume), *Memoirs of Hope* (Weidenfeld and Nicolson, London, 1971).

The Speeches of General de Gaulle (Oxford University Press, London, 1942).

Speeches of General de Gaulle, Vol. 2 (Oxford University Press, London, 1943).

Discours et messages du Général de Gaulle, ed. F. Goguel (Plon, Paris, 1970–1, 5 vols.)

Works about de Gaulle and Gaullism

Aglion, R., *Roosevelt and de Gaulle; Allies in Conflict. A Personal Memoir* (Collier Macmillan, London, 1988).

Blanc, P.-L., *De Gaulle au soir de sa vie* (Fayard, Paris, 1990).

Cerny, P. G., *The Politics of Grandeur. Ideological Aspects of de Gaulle's Foreign Policy* (Cambridge University Press, 1980).

Charlot, J., *L'Union pour la Nouvelle République. Etude du pouvoir au sein d'un parti politique* (Colin, Paris, 1967).

Charlot, J., *The Gaullist Phenomenon: The Gaullist Movement in the Fifth Republic* (1970; English translation: Allen and Unwin, London, 1971).

Charlot, J., *Le Gaullisme d' opposition 1946–1958: histoire politique du gaullisme* (Fayard, Paris, 1983).

Cook, D., *Charles de Gaulle. A Biography* (Secker and Warburg, London, 1984).

Courtois, S. and Lazar, M. (eds.), *Cinquante ans d'une passion française. De Gaulle et les communistes* (Balland, Paris, 1991).

Duhamel, A. *De Gaulle–Mitterand. La marque et la trace* (Flammarion, Paris, 1991).

Hartley, A., *Gaullism: the Rise and Fall of a Political Movement* (Routledge and Kegan Paul, London, 1972).

Jackson, J., *Charles de Gaulle* (Cardinal, London, 1990).

Kersaudy, F., *Churchill and de Gaulle* (Collins, London, 1981).

Lacouture, J., *De Gaulle* (1984–6, 3 vols.); English translation, *De Gaulle* (London, Collins-Harvill, 1990–1, in 2 vols.); Vol. 1 *The Rebel 1890–1944* (1990); Vol. 2 *The Ruler 1945–1970* (1991).

Ledwidge, B., *De Gaulle* (Weidenfeld and Nicolson, London, 1982).

Malraux, A., *Fallen Oaks. Conversation with de Gaulle* (1971; English translation: Hamish Hamilton, London, 1972).

Mauriac, C., *De Gaulle* (1964; English translation: Bodley Head, London, 1966).

Mauriac, C., *The Other de Gaulle. Diaries 1944–1954* (1971; English translation: Angus and Robertson, London, 1973).

Purtschet, C., *Le Rassemblement du Peuple Français, 1947–1953* (Editions Cujas, Paris, 1965).

Rémond, R., *Le Retour de De Gaulle* (Editions Complexe, Brussels, 1987).

Rudelle, O., *Mai 1958, de Gaulle et la République* (Plon, Paris, 1988).

Shennan, A., *De Gaulle* (Longman, Harlow, 1993)

Touchard, J., *Le Gaullisme 1940–1969* (Seuil, Paris, 1978).

Tournoux, J. R., *Pétain and de Gaulle* (1964; English translation: Heinemann, London, 1966).

Werth, A., *De Gaulle; a Political Biography* (Penguin, London, 1967).

White, D. S., *Black Africa and De Gaulle. From the French Empire to Independence* (Pennsylvania State University Press, University Park, Penn.,1979).

Contextual Works

Azéma, J.-P., *From Munich to the Liberation 1938–1944* (1979; English translation: Cambridge University Press, 1984).

Azéma, J.-P., *1940. L' année terrible* (Seuil, Paris, 1990).

Berstein, S., *La France de l' expansion*, Vol. 1 *La République gaullienne 1958–1969* (Seuil, Paris, 1989).

Crozier, M., *The Stalled Society* (1970; English translation: Viking Press, New York, 1973).

Hamon, H., and Rotman, P., *Génération*, Vol. 1 *Les Années de rêve* (Seuil, Paris, 1987); Vol. 2 *Les Années de poudre* (Seuil, Paris, 1988).

Hoffmann, S., *Decline or Renewal? France since the 1930s* (Viking, New York, 1974).

Larkin, M., *France since the Popular Front. Government and People 1936–1986* (Clarendon Press, Oxford, 1988).

Maier, C. S. and White, D. S., *The Thirteenth of May. The Advent of de Gaulle's Republic* (Oxford University Press, New York, 1968).

Rioux, J.-P., *The Fourth Republic 1944–1958* (1980; English translation: Cambridge University Press, 1987).

Rioux, J.-P. (ed.), *La Guerre d' Algérie et les français* (Fayard, Paris, 1990).

Rousso, H., *The Vichy Syndrome. History and Memory in France since 1944* (1987; English translation: Harvard University Press, Cambridge, Mass., 1991).

Williams, P. and Harrison, M., *Politics and Society in de Gaulle's Republic* (Longman, Harlow, 1971).

Winock, M., *La République se meurt. Chronique 1956–1958* (Seuil, Paris, 1978).

Winock, M., *Chronique des années soixante* (Seuil, Paris, 1987).

Index